Strategy in His Image: Supporting and Sustaining Organizational Strategy From a Christian Perspective

Strategy in His Image: Supporting and Sustaining Organizational Strategy From a Christian Perspective

Joe M. Ricks, Jr.
Richard Peters

≡IAP

INFORMATION AGE PUBLISHING, INC.
Charlotte, NC • www.infoagepub.com

Library of Congress Cataloging-In-Publication Data

The CIP data for this book can be found on the Library of Congress website (loc.gov).

Paperback: 979-8-88730-245-4
Hardcover: 979-8-88730-246-1
E-Book: 979-8-88730-247-8

CONTENTS

FOREWORD

Slade Simons
Gulf Coast Wealth Management

Years ago, I was sitting in a Bible Study teacher training session and our pastor taught us that we were going to build our teaching and education program with three main pillars: knowledge, understanding, and wisdom. He went on to define each in the following way: knowledge is knowing what the Bible says, understanding is knowing what it means, and wisdom is knowing how to apply it. What I came to learn is that we can have all of the knowledge and all of the understanding, but if we don't have wisdom, if we don't know how to apply that which we know and understand, then we will likely bear no fruit.

Dr. Ricks and Dr. Peters have put forth a book to help produce the fruit that comes from practical wisdom. This book is not a "how to guide." This is a strategic thinking guide. We live in a world today that is heavily populated with videos on how to do anything in minutes. Millions of people, of which I am one, rely on these videos to learn new things and fix existing problems. The simplicity that comes with these videos is both useful and satisfying. Yet, its genius of simplicity is not completely transferable, particularly when it comes to matters of business, and strategy.

Strategy in His Image challenges the intellect. It challenges the heart and the motive. It challenges "the why." Dr. Ricks and Dr. Peters present their case and give readers the room to develop their own conclusion, for there is no one right

Strategy in His Image: Supporting and Sustaining Organizational Strategy
From a Christian Perspective, pages vii–ix.
Copyright © 2023 by Information Age Publishing
www.infoagepub.com

answer in the forum of strategic thinking. They balance academia with practical real-world ideas and do so all within the context of Biblical teachings.

I am a Christian and have been for the past 30 years. Since I graduated from college, I have spent my entire working life in the business world. I am currently responsible for two divisions of the company I work for and serve as a board member and leader for a few different non-profits in our community. I love strategic thinking and am a huge believer in planning. I was taught many years ago to plan your work and then work your plan. I learned that planning increases the probability of success. And I also learned that things happen in life that cause us to change our plans so it would be wise to commit to the goal and not to the plan. As Dr. Ricks and Dr. Peters note, remaining faithful while flexible is challenging, but not novel.

Strategic planning is a multi-billion dollar business that gets a tremendous amount of time and attention in the world of commerce. I am one of its greatest advocates and one of its loyal consumers and users. Every year, I go through a strategic planning process for the divisions that I lead, the company I work for, the church that I'm a member of, and the non-profits where I serve. In any given year, I participate in four to five different strategic planning conversations. I thoroughly enjoy the reflection and discussion around our strengths, weaknesses, opportunities, and threats (commonly referred to as S.W.O.T. analysis). I am often energized by the thoughts and dreams of what can be accomplished in the future. Yet, I have come to learn over the years that my strategic plan can be reduced to an annual exercise that results in an excellent starting point, but one that can be derailed a bit with unexpected events throughout the year. I have also learned that strategic planning and the plan itself can quickly become about results. And, as many in business have learned (often the hard way), we can't always control outcomes.

Strategic planning often involves some form of competitive analysis where we look at what the competition is doing, where they are having success, and if there is something we should be doing to combat their actions. Dr. Ricks and Dr. Peters remind us that strategic thinking is not a copy-cat business. Strategic thinking, as laid out in this book, allows the individual and the group to reflect and contemplate all that is before them with a construct that goes far beyond the common S.W.O. T. analysis. For those who follow Christ, it allows us the opportunity to pray and hear from God, to read the scripture, and to discern what He is calling us to do in our business, ministry, and community service. Dr. Ricks and Dr. Peters present the scripture as a guiding light for direction, but leave the path open to us, the reader, by challenging us with thought provoking concepts, such as Subsidiarity with solidarity. This was a tough concept for me to understand and grasp at the first read (and I hope it is for you too). I had to read and reread this section a few times, but each time I did, I learned more and could see specific examples of application in my professional work, as well as in the work that I am part of as a layman in church. Throughout the book they presented questions and ideas such as,

- To what degree do our workplace actions affect God's Kingdom and even God Himself?
- In market driven economies like the United States, strategic business decisions not only have major implications for the profitability and sustainability of the organization and its stakeholders, but these decisions also have major implications on the access to goods and services for God's creation—its people.
- This tension between pure and profitable Christianity is one that seems destined to undermine discussions and, more importantly, the implementation of workplace spirituality.
- Stewardship requires individuals to view resources and opportunities as charges that require dutiful management and preservation, in order to promote sustainability and social well-being.

Being a Christian who is responsible for leading a division is both a privilege and a struggle. There are times when I am required to make complex decisions and I feel the conviction to stay true to my faith at the same time. I have talked with other Christian leaders, and it seems very common for us to wonder how our professional careers fit within our Christian walks. Leadership can come with praise, but it can also come with criticism and second-guessing by those who have been asked or assigned to follow. Clarity of mission and conviction, along with clarity of communication are two of the most important elements of leadership. This clarity often comes from time spent strategically thinking.

Throughout this book, I made notes, underlined statements, and put question marks in the margin. I thought through their ideas and looked up the scriptures. This is the blessing of this book. It is not about answers. It's about strategically thinking through the lens of Biblical teaching and real-world application. It is about building our knowledge, growing in our understanding, and exercising wisdom.

PREFACE

As business scholars and practicing Christians we believed there had to be a Biblically based Christian spiritual model that business leaders generally and Christian leaders specifically can use for their strategic thinking and concluded that it was our responsibility to develop it.

HOW WE GOT HERE:

With my work is strategic philanthropy and Richard's in social responsibility and sustainability we had published a few papers together and had a number of conversations about our research interests along with many other topics including our faith. During one of our conversations Richard had just read Maybe et. al. (2016) "Having Burned the Straw Man of Christian Spiritual Leadership, what can We Learn from Jesus About Leading Ethically?" and asked me to look at it and let him know what I thought. This ask was the start of the conversation that eventually lead to this project.

We reached the same conclusion regarding Maybe and his colleagues' work. Through our conversations we concluded that we agreed with their conclusion that in the published research largely under the label of Spirituality at Work (SAW) or Spiritual Leadership (SL,) the 'Christianity' of Christian business lead-

Strategy in His Image: Supporting and Sustaining Organizational Strategy
From a Christian Perspective, pages xi–xiii.
Copyright © 2023 by Information Age Publishing
www.infoagepub.com
All rights of reproduction in any form reserved.

ership is often missing and at times actually is incongruent with the teachings of Jesus Christ. However, we also agreed that Mabey and his colleagues 'threw the baby out with the bath water' by positioning Jesus Centered Leadership (JCL) as contrary, rather than complementary, to established organizational approaches. We also concluded that if JCL and other future spiritual paradigms do not integrate conventional business goals, knowledge, and institutional stakeholders they will remain as ideals on the fringes of business strategy and will have limited usefulness even to Christian business leaders. Our conclusions were simply that the current SAW and SL literature was not enough for Christian leaders and the research that tried to correct this was too disconnected from business realities to be useful. As business scholars and practicing Christians we believed there had to be a Biblically based Christian spiritual model that business leaders in general and Christian leaders specifically can use for their strategic thinking and we believed that it was our responsibility to develop it.

We started with a journal article "Jesus-Centered Leadership and Business Applications: An Alternative Approach" to introduce our model. Due to space limitations and the review process, we weren't able to expand on the model to the extent we wished. Then an RFP came across my desk for chapters in an edited book: Blessed are Those Who Ask the Questions, a volume in the series Contemporary perspectives in management, spirituality and religion. This project gave us the opportunity to expand our original manuscript, and we produced a chapter "The strategy of spirituality: How best can spiritual leadership and spirituality at work support and sustain organizational strategy: A Christian perspective?" Even with the additional creative license and expanded space there was still a lot of work to be done especially regarding the theological and biblical rational for our model. It was from these thoughts the idea for Strategy in His Image was conceived.

WHAT WE WISH TO ACCOMPLISH NOW:

Our goal as business scholars and practicing Christians is to contribute a faith-inspired, biblically based perspective that is consistent with the needs of strategic-organizational leadership. Neither of us are theological scholars, however we use our training as business scholars to examine the theology literature as well as business scholarship to build a model based on sound Christian principles with sound business applications. The theological rational for our model is based on our understanding and interpretation of key scriptures in addition to a discussion of creations relationship with and responsibility to God. We directly address criticisms of capitalism and for profit business and present a model that we believe is not only biblical but also comprehensible and actionable within the context of strategic thinking for business organizations.

Even though we rely heavily on the academic literature in business and theology, we are very intentional on making this a practitioner focused book. While we are confident academics and researchers will see a contribution to the literature and that it has classroom value, this was written with the Christian businessperson in mind. The person that must often make business decisions and wants to stay true to their faith. The person that sometimes wonder how or even if their professional career fits with their Christian walk.

THANK YOU TO:

First, we'd like to thank God for giving us the ability, purpose, and direction for integrating our professional work and our faith. This has been one of the most fulfilling projects of our careers. Second, thank you to our families for their support and inspiration: our wives Dianne Way-Ricks and Brittany Bloom Peters; our children Jaelynn Ricks and Jude, Liam, Pierce, and Kiersten Peters; and all of our family members and supporters near and far. We'd like to offer a special thanks to our editor Norman Stovall, DACO LLC for the design of our cover, and to those that offered feedback and review of our work. Thank you: Rev. Mitchell Stevenson, Landon Bishop, Ralph Johnson, Min. Anthony Smith, Whitney Brown, Slade Simons, Nathan Eberline, Dr. Jose Bautista, Pastor Chip Luter, and Pastor Fred Luter, Jr.

CHAPTER 1

INTRODUCTION

In market driven economies like the United States, strategic-business decisions not only have major implication for the profitability and sustainability of the organization and its stakeholders, these decisions also have major implications on the access to goods and services for God's creation—its people.

Spiritual Leadership and Spirituality at Work are significant themes of contemporary business literature that have offered an alternative approach to doing business by focusing on spiritual development, faith, and morality in the workplace. With pervasive concern for morality and social responsibility to not only influence but to also guide centrally the efforts of organizations' traditional taboo themes such as religion, righteousness and reverence are increasingly intersecting with issues of relevance (with respect to work and/or authority) and reward (financial and otherwise). While the spirituality literature is significant only a small segment looks at spirituality specifically through a Christian lens. This work is intended to address spirituality from a Christian perspective. As business scholars and practicing Christians, we believe we can contribute a faith-inspired, biblically based perspective that is consistent with the needs of strategic-organizational leadership. We see our role consistent with evangelical discipleship as well as Catholic social tradition, where it is the responsibility of the laity to bring the

Strategy in His Image: Supporting and Sustaining Organizational Strategy From a Christian Perspective, pages 1–9.
Copyright © 2023 by Information Age Publishing
www.infoagepub.com

gospel to the homes, schools, and workplaces of the secular world.[1] Neither of us is a theological scholar, however we will delve into theological and business scholarship to build a model to articulate sound Christian principles with sound business applications.

While we speak to spirituality quite a bit, it is only because there has been a great deal of work on the concept of spirituality in the literature by business scholars and we use this work to help build our model based on Christian principles. While some might disagree about the promotion of spirituality in the workplace, there seems to be broad agreement by business scholars and practitioners on the increased need for business ethics—organizationally, societally, and from a sense of strategic-organizational leadership. Our model looks at how principles grounded in Christian faith help accomplish this goal. Workers seeking a sovereign's calling, managers striving for servanthood-type leadership, and organizations supplying supportive environments all suggest that firms can harmoniously integrate purpose and profit.

A more empowered workforce, enlightened management, and an embracing workplace should lead to conventional ingredients of success: efficiency and effectiveness.

However, inevitably many firms find it both impractical and/or implausible to fully commit to the tenets of workplace spirituality. We posit that this unwillingness or inability stems from two conflicts inherent in our present treatment of spirituality in business:

1. Spirituality that 'fits' with conventional business models and applications is not spiritual enough and compromises its religiosity for financial reward.
2. Perspectives that try to correct this; those that prioritize the normative over the instrumental, are irreconcilable with most strategic thinking and therefore unfeasible to implement.

Ironically, both conflicts often lead to the same unfortunate consequence; the relegation of spirituality to the fringes or grassroots of business. Without resolution, this is where it is likely to stay, gaining little actual legitimacy and leverage from corporate decision-makers.

As difficult as it may seem, we believe it is critical for organizations to reconcile workplace spirituality with strategic thinking and business operations, as religious identity is still very important in the United States. Data from the latest Pew Research Center shows 77% of Americans self-identify with an established faith (Pew Research Center).[2] Identity is formed by the interaction of two components: structure and agency. Structure involves the external factors that influence

---

[1] Kennedy, R. (2012) *The good that business does*. Acton Institute.
[2] Pew Research Center. Retrieved 04/20/2018 from: http://www.pewforum.org/religious-landscape-study/.

identity, while agency involves one's freedom of choice.[3] Even if organizations try to create religion-free structures, where work is work and not a place for personal beliefs, this will at minimum create conflict within the individual agent or employee that has chosen to identify as a Christian. Evidence suggests that the conflict between individual faith and the workplace is already taking place and finding its way to the judicial system. Employment discrimination claims based on religion rose 82% between 1992 to 2003. These claims have come from a broad spectrum of faith groups from small poorly understood groups to Catholics and Evangelicals.[4]

We see the task of providing a faith-inspired, biblically based perspective to practicing Christian business leaders as critical, particularly in countries like the United States, where the vast majority of the population identifies as Christian. When engaging in business or any non-religious activity, the Christian perspective must not only be biblical, it must also be comprehensible and actionable within the context of the said activity. In a for-profit business context the Christian perspective must be biblical and allow for profits; this is the only way Christians can operate or have any influence in the for-profit business world. If Christianity did not allow for profits, Christians could not exist in the for-profit world; it would be incomprehensible and non-actionable. In the case of business, where we seek to contribute, not only do we see Christianity being important to business strategy and operations, we also see biblical evidence that business strategy and operations may be of significant importance to Christianity.

Using Jesus' references to work roles and work-related activity, we can conclude that work and the workplace were very important to Jesus. Issler explored work related references used in the parables Jesus used to communicate to his followers. According to Issler 32 parables mention some form of labor related activity, and the estimated number of parables Jesus used will vary from 37 to 75 depending on how one defines a parable.[5] Using this range, Jesus references work in somewhere between forty-two and eighty-six percent of his parables. Beyond the examining of Jesus' parables, scripture presents us with a more fundamental question relevant to the question of Christianity in the workplace: To what degree do our workplace actions affect God's Kingdom or even God himself?

In "The Openness of God: A Biblical Challenge to the Traditional Understanding of God" (1994) Pinnock and his colleagues introduce their "openness" model into the theological debate regarding the nature of God and the free will of man. They argue through different lenses conservative, moderate, and progressive theology views regarding the nature of God, specifically, some of his attributes in-

---

[3] Collins, J. C., & Porras, J. I. (1994). *Built to last: Successful habits of visionary companies.* Harper Business.

[4] Foltin, R., & Standish, J. (2004). Reconciling faith and livelihood: Religion in the workplace and Title VII. *Human Rights, 31*, 19–24.

[5] Issler, K. (2014). Exploring the pervasive references to Jesus' parables. *Journal of Theological Society, 57*, 323–339.

cluding: immutability, timelessness, omnipotence, and exhaustive foreknowledge. Though all would argue for the free will of man to some degree, the lens from which one views God's nature has a significant effect on the degree of freedom in the free will of man.[6] Regardless of the theological perspective, one's views on the relationship between man's free will and God's nature will shape one's perspectives and positions on his or her role in business decisions and strategy.

The conservative view constricts free will the most. Generally speaking, in the conservative view, God is completely unchanging and immovable. All of creation will adhere to God's will in the end. No matter what man does, God's will is set and must be done. Man's decisions can cause things to be thrown off course a bit, or they may delay the inevitable, but in the end man's decisions don't matter. The progressive view, usually identified with process theology, gives the free will of man the ultimate freedom. In fact, in process theology God is constricted by man as God is ontologically dependent on the world. Progressiveness is exemplified by the theology of Paul Tullich. According to Tullich, God is Being-Itself and the biblical actions of God are descriptions of our participation in Being-Itself; God is immanent with man's living and acting. Moderate views like the openness model give man full freedom of will and restricts God only in the view that God chose to give man free will in order to have a loving relationship, where one can choose to accept or reject God. In giving man free will God made the execution of his will somewhat dependent on the actions of man.[7]

What is clear from Pinnock et al's analysis is that if you believe man has any amount of free will, no matter the lens, the actions of man have at least some effect on God's plan. If one holds the conservative view, you do not want to be the one to delay God's plan, even if you believe it to be inevitable. If one holds a moderate or open view, man's actions have a direct effect on God's actions and the execution of God's plan. In the process view, man's actions and God's actions appear to be one and the same. Our model extends from a moderate or open perspective, understanding these classifications is important because man as God's partner in the open view is foundational for our thesis.

In market driven economies like the United States, strategic-business decisions not only have major implications for the profitability and sustainability of the organization and its stakeholders, these decisions also have major implications on the access to goods and services for God's creation—its people. In the vast majority of cases where we have a need, we have to buy something in the marketplace in order to meet our need, therefore pricing and distribution decisions among others have a direct effect on the ability of people to access goods and services to meet their needs. In the description of the last judgement: Matthew 25:31–46, particularly verses 35–43, Jesus clearly teaches us that we have a responsibility to provide for the needs of our fellow man:

---

[6] Pinnock, C., Rice, R., Sanders, J., Hasker, W., & Basinger, D. (1994). *The openness of God A: biblical challenge to the traditional understanding of God.* InterVarsity Press.
[7] Ibid. 91–98.

Then the King will say to those on His right hand, 'Come, you blessed of My Father, inherit the kingdom prepared for you from the foundation of the world: [35] for I was hungry and you gave Me food; I was thirsty and you gave Me drink; I was a stranger and you took Me in; [36] I *was* naked and you clothed Me; I was sick and you visited Me; I was in prison and you came to Me.' [37] "Then the righteous will answer Him, saying, 'Lord, when did we see You hungry and feed *You,* or thirsty and give *You* drink? [38] When did we see You a stranger and take *You* in, or naked and clothe *You?* [39] Or when did we see You sick, or in prison, and come to You?' [40] And the King will answer and say to them, 'Assuredly, I say to you, in as much as you did *it* to one of the least of these My brethren, you did *it* to Me.' [41] "Then He will also say to those on the left hand, Depart from Me, you cursed, into the everlasting fire prepared for the devil and his angels: [42] for I was hungry and you gave Me no food; I was thirsty and you gave Me no drink; [43] I was a stranger and you did not take Me in, naked and you did not clothe Me, sick and in prison and you did not visit Me' (NKJV).

Christians that are organizational leaders, tasked with the responsibility of sustaining their organizations as well as the duty of meeting the needs of God's creation, have an extremely complex task. To address this complexity, we argue for a faith-inspired, biblically based perspective that values and utilizes the benefits of Christian spirituality, while simultaneously advocating for existing strategic thinking. We do not suggest that either (strategy or Christianity) should be prioritized over the other. Instead, we outline and discuss biblically based alternatives that aim to reconcile the 'differences' and effectively merge these together and, essentially build the bridge between Christianity and capitalism. We believe that using biblical principles to guide strategic decision making will give business leaders the opportunity to simultaneously practice their professions and their faiths. Again, we see this as critical because in capitalist economies, all of God's creation—Christian or not—get most of their needs met through marketplace exchanges.

In his discussion and critique of the theology of Tullich, Thiselton asks "Is it possible for the theologian to live in faith and doubt simultaneously?" This challenge to Tullich's theology speaks to the difficulty of maintaining a consistent theological idea in a natural perceived and observed world.[8] While theologians have the luxury of time to study, pray, meditate, and ponder these questions, practicing Christians with everyday job responsibilities do not. Practicing Christians with everyday job responsibilities cannot ask the question: Can one be a Christian and a capitalist simultaneously? They have to ask the question: How can I be an effective Christian and a capitalist simultaneously?

We're sure that history is replete with examples of practicing Christians having to figure out how to integrate faith into important secular strategic decisions. We find one of the most interesting to be King James and the development of the King James translation of the English Bible, and the related use of the King James

---

[8] Thiselton, A. C. *The theology of Paul Tillich.* Church Society. https://churchsociety.org/docs/churchman/088/Cman_088_2_Thiselton.pdf

and Geneva translations by the seventeenth century pilgrims in America. In his book, "God's Secretaries the Making of the King James Bible," Adam Nicolson details the story of the reasoning and process for the development of the King James translation of the Bible[9]. King James came to power in England during a time of significant challenges. First, there was the increasingly unpopular war with Spain and the financial burden it was placing on England. Additionally, and more relevant to this work, there was a significant religious war between three separate factions: (1) Roman Catholics who wanted England to be a part of the Roman Catholic Church under the control of the pope, (2) the Puritans that did not see the Church of England as true representation of the Reformation, and (3) those that supported the Church of England.[10] It was at a conference at Hampton Court to discuss and debate the issues regarding the Church of England where the idea of the King James translation of the Bible was born.[11]

The primary purpose for the development of the King James translation of the Bible was nation building. King James sought to create a compromise between the Church of England (Bishops Bible) and English Protestants (Geneva Bible) in order to unite England. When the pilgrims arrived in America the Bible of choice was the Calvin-translated Geneva Bible. The language of the Geneva Bible was inherently contentious between a vengeful God and worldly government and worked well with the early founders in their separation from England and establishment of America. However, as the country expanded and matured, the need for the practical application of nation building made the King James Bible the standard bearer of early America to the extent that most American Christians have never even heard of the Geneva Bible[12].

King James and his decision to create his translation in such a way as to unite a nation and the early pilgrims landing with the Geneva Bible, moving to the King James Bible as the society evolved both demonstrate the challenge and the responsibility of practicing Christians in positions of authority. Christian leaders of countries, societies, or organizations that affect the lives of God's people have an obligation to continuously examine their theology in the context of their responsibility to the countries, societies, and organizations they lead. King James and the early pilgrims were in a position where they had to make strategic decisions while attempting to keep their faith intact.

This example is instructional for two important reasons. The first is that theology and Christianity has direct strategic influence on how institutions, like firms, are organized and governed. Secondly, scriptures provide important organizational stakeholders with practical guidelines to pursue in an effort to promote individual and collective performance. Thus, theology and faith adopt a greater role in the implementation and outcomes of a business. It is not merely an overly-

---

[9] Nicolson, A. (2003). *God's secretaries the making of the King James Bible.* Harper Collins.
[10] Ibid. 2–3.
[11] Ibid. 42.
[12] Ibid. 229–230.

ing, abstract value system, but a key component and tool to tailor organizational practices, task organizational stakeholders, and transform organizational mindsets in a manner that promotes strategic performance (financial and otherwise).

This is of course a positivist interpretation that can be criticized by those who view any attempt to invoke and integrate scripture into strategy as sacrilegious and sinful. Arguably, King James' actions could be positioned as political expedience proffered by scriptural manipulations. That cynicism is challenging to overcome, but acts as one motivation for our writing this book. Through our model and discussions, we hope to invoke serious thought about the strategic usefulness of God's word. As the model seeks to inspire readers to consider why and how capitalism and Christianity can symbiotically coexist, especially in a society acutely aware of the dangers of untampered markets and corporate greed. Further, we attempt to instigate debate that moves us from the dialectic of simple moral vs. economic to a discourse rich in the intertwining of scripture and strategy.

As we make our arguments, it will be obvious that along with the spirituality literature our empirical, as well as a number of our conceptual arguments are based in the literature on ethics and corporate social responsibility (CSR). We recognize that all ethical and socially responsible concepts are not Christian; ethics and social consciousness are necessary, but insufficient for Christianity. However, we do rely on the premise that organizations with these foundational concepts are those where Christian faith and business strategy are likely to thrive. Additionally, it is our belief that for biblical concepts to be intelligible in applied disciplines like strategy those concepts must be integrated and discussed in ways that are coherent and understood by those in that discipline. Pinnock, in discussing the existential fit of the openness theology makes this point quite eloquently and succinctly, "Ideas have consequences and beliefs affect behavior. It is important, therefore, that doctrines are credible in practical terms as well as biblically and rationally sound. They ought to have a ring of truth and make a difference in life. They ought to be relevant to real life situations and motivate us and effect how we live."[13] We believe the integration of sound theology with these particular research streams will allow us to build a relevant and motivating model. Stated another way, we argue for biblically based principles for strategic thought, not necessarily to evangelize our faith, but because we believe they are sound and in the best interest of individuals, organizations, and society.

In the chapters that follow, we review the evolution of the spirituality and spirituality at work literature as well as the limited literature that examines these concepts from a Christian perspective. During the review we identify significant obstacles that have thus far kept these concepts on the fringes of general management thinking and practices. While purportedly prioritizing personal value and Christ-like attributes, these obstacles however present challenges to managing organizations, especially those that adopt a religious and/or moral approach to

---

[13] Pinnock, C. (2001). *Most moved mover: A theology of God's openness.* Backer Academic.

business enterprise. After identifying the challenges associated with a Christian approach to the spirituality literature, we offer the model shown in Figure 1.1 with four principles for Strategic Spirituality based on a Christian perspective of biblical interpretations. These principles offer the requisite pragmatism for strategic thinking and organizational implementation. The four principles include:

1. *Subsidiarity with Solidarity*—Subsidiarity is a principle of decentralization coming for the Catholic social tradition whereby decision-making done at the organizational level with the greatest familiarity and individual empowerment. It prioritizes the value of individuals as gifted and talented human beings. Subsidiarity is moderated by solidarity or a unity of common mission.

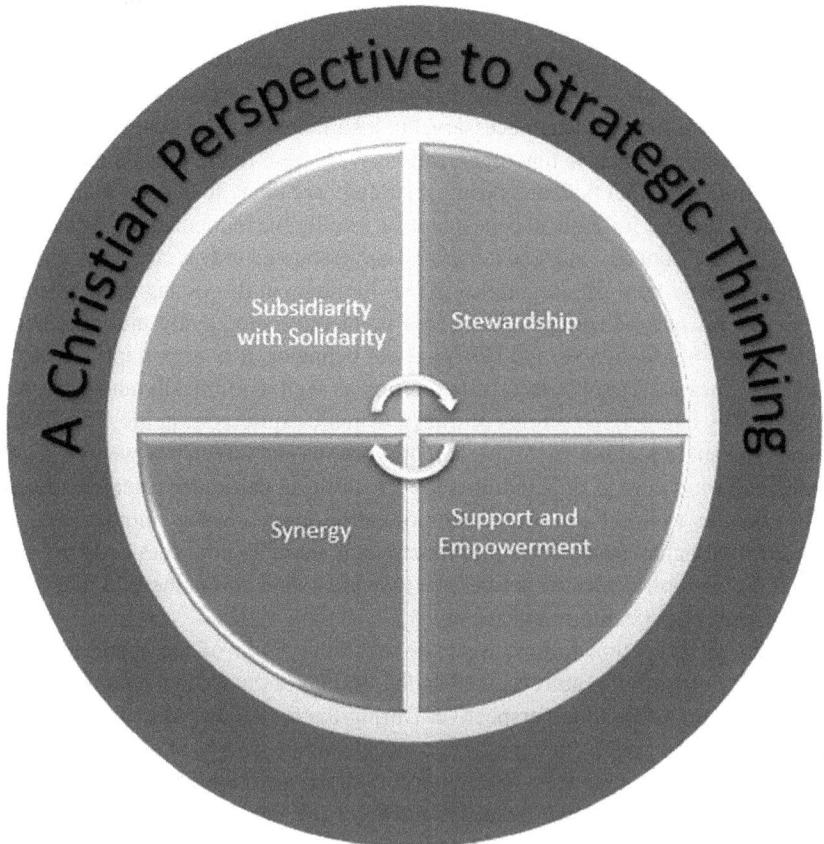

FIGURE 1.1.

2. *Stewardship*—requires resources and opportunities be dutifully managed in order to promote sustainability and social well-being.

3. *Support and Empowerment*—relates to the creation of an organization with Christian principles where Christians and Non-Christians are supported and empowered for individual growth and organizational success.

4. *Synergy*—allows organizations to remain focused on their ideals but flexible in their implementation.

These, as noted previously, are offered as guiding principles for organizational strategizing and leadership. While their application may be nuanced, we purposely chose these because we believe in their universality and their ability to be executed even with the idiosyncrasies of institutions and organizational environments. Additionally, we consider these principles individually, but argue that they are reinforced through simultaneous engagement. For example, we posit that the delegation that is central to subsidiarity is best engineered through subordinate support, which in turn catalyzes synergistic potential within the organization. And although it is possible that some cascading or organic effect may materialize (i.e. synergy naturally occurs support), we propose that it is essential for leaders to be intentional about all of these principles individually as well as collectively. As a whole, they contribute to an organization that thinks and acts in a strategic way and consistent with the Christian faith.

CHAPTER 2

SPIRITUALITY LITERATURE AND CHRISTIANITY

Commonality and Contention

This is undoubtedly conceptually appealing but implementing leadership and strategy that is based on these lofty ideals lacks the necessary pragmatism to be actionable in a business environment.

SPIRITUALITY LITERATURE AND CHRISTIANITY: COMMONALITY AND CONTENTION

A book like this is not a legitimization of Christianity, Christian Leadership, or even Christian Capitalism. Instead, it is a testament of the reality that faith often converges with the demands of the secular work environment at the individual, group, and organizational levels.[1]

---

[1] Brown, R. B. (2003). Organizational spirituality: The sceptic's version. *Organization, 10,* 393–400. Jossey-Bass. Neal, J. A., & Bennett, J. (2000). Examining multi-level or holistic spiritual phenomena in the work place. *Management, Spirituality, & Religion Newsletter, Academy of Management,* (Winter), 1–2. Lewis, J. S., & Geroy, G. D. (2000). Employee spirituality in the workplace: A cross-cultural view for the management of spiritual employees. *Journal of Management Education, 24,* 682–694.

As the data in the introductory chapter suggest, religious belief is still valued by many working Americans, which strongly suggests that people want to integrate rather than isolate their Christian values from their careers.[2] Also, anecdotal and empirical information may actually encourage organizations not only to welcome, but also to actually leverage spirituality for its positive influences on important organizational outcomes, like commitment and culture. [3]

But using God to generate organizational goodwill and ultimately gain can raise suspicion and uneasiness in even the strongest of workplace spirituality advocates. Leaders, even well-intentioned ones, can find themselves becoming precariously closer to behavior that may be seen as deceptive. While the mantra 'do it for Jesus" is potentially more spiritually correct, it may also be more politically coercive and managers instead of motivating employees, are accused of manipulating them in the pursuit of financial gain and glory.[4]

This tension between pure and profitable Christianity is one that seems destined to undermine discussions and more importantly the implementation of workplace spirituality. There are those that consider any attempt at mixing religion and riches as sacrilegious, but this view is arguably in the minority, especially in contemporary society, and especially in the Western world. More popular, but thus far harder to prove or prevent is the perspective that spirituality at work and spiritual leadership have been rampantly misused and abused by those who seek their own agenda of avarice. Therefore, it is not the outcome of financial gain that is anti-Jesus, but it is the methods that prioritize manipulation, monopolize individual thought and/or idolize material gain that are.[5] To lead like Jesus is to be open to opposition, to place service over superiority, and to pursue love at all costs, even financial costs.

Mitroff, I. A., & Denton, E. A. (1999). A spiritual audit of corporate America: A hard look at spirituality, religion, and values in the workplace.

[2] Mitroff, I. (2003). Do not promote religion under the guise of spirituality. *Organization, 10*, 375–382. Mitroff, I. A., & Denton, E. A. (1999). *A spiritual audit of corporate America: A hard look at spirituality, religion, and values in the workplace.*, Jossey-Bass.

[3] Bell, E. (2008). Towards a critical spirituality of organization. *Culture and Organization, 3*, 293–307. Berret-Koehler. Kraimer, M. L. (1997). Organization goals and values: a socialization model. *Human Resource Management Review, 7*, 425–448. Collins, J. C., & Porras, J. I. (1994). *Built to last: Successful habits of visionary companies.* Harper Business. Hawley, J. (1993). Reawaking the spirit in work: the power of dharmic management. Milliman, J., Czaplewski, A. J. & Ferguson, J. (2003). Workplace spirituality and employee work attitudes: An exploratory empirical assessment. *Journal of Organizational Change Management, 16*, 426–447. Neck, C. P., & Milliman, J. F. (1994). Thought self-leadership: finding spiritual fulfillment in organizational life. *Journal of Managerial Psychology, 9*, 9–16.

[4] Driscoll, C., & Wiebe, E. (2007). *Technical spirituality at work: Jacques Ellul on workplace spirituality.* Academy of Management Meeting, 2007, Philadelphia.

[5] Mabey, C., Conroy, M., Blakeley, K, & de Marco, S. (2016). Having burned the straw man of Christian spiritual leadership, what can we Learn from Jesus about leading ethically? *Journal of Business Ethics.* doi:10.1007/s10551-016-3054-5

This is undoubtedly conceptually appealing but implementing leadership and strategy that is based on these lofty ideals lacks the necessary pragmatism to be actionable in a business environment. Even advocates of this position provide few practical examples of these virtues in action. What 'evidence' is provided is limited to those organizations or individuals that are explicit in the Christian faith; essentially those that are faith-based rather than based on faith. The former includes only a very small sub-set of all organizational entities worldwide. It is the latter though that are likely to represent a burgeoning body of entities that desire to achieve success through principal purposes and processes. But while many authors share why this approach is good (or the converse is troublesome), there is little prescriptive advice as to how to best achieve what we term 'spiritually strategic' outcomes.

We posit that these outcomes do not merely occur from good intentions and/or virtuous behavior. Instead, they must be meticulously managed since this version of workplace spirituality can be particularly antithetical to traditional markets, organization motives, and general management. This may explain why constructs like business ethics and corporate social responsibility, though reasonably mature in corporate circles, are still to be fully and genuinely embraced by the rank and file. The fact remains that despite all our suppositions about synergy, symbiosis, and/or shared value, Christian leadership does not readily or easily co-exist with corporate activity. Let's consider one element of proposed Christian Leadership; being regulated from within rather than externally. This is often touted as the hallmark characteristic of the most ethical and socially responsible organizations and one distinctive element that explains why these organizations benefit most from their virtuous values. The assumption is that there is no competitive advantage to be gained from compliance. Thus, if firms do the minimum (i.e. comply) there is minimal opportunity for competitive separation. This may ultimately be true, but there is enough published research that counters the proposition that doing more good is strategically or even spiritually advantageous for the firms. Further, there is ample evidence to suggest that firms who are overly discretionary in their spiritual stance (without careful and cautious consideration of their external stakeholders) may be forced to backtrack.

This isn't simply a case of being reviled for acting righteously, but a recognition that righteousness is often predicated on the needs of others rather than one's own desires. In Matthew 23:13–36 Jesus himself chastises the scribes and Pharisees for invoking their own goals of goodness rather than attending to those in their audiences. Particularly in Matthew 23: 23 when Jesus states "Woe to you, scribes and Pharisees, hypocrites! For you pay tithe of mint and anise and cumin, and have neglected the weightier matters of the law: justice and mercy and faith. These you ought to have done, without leaving the others undone" (NKJV). These leaders prioritized the giving of earthly tithes over what Jesus termed the 'weightier matters' like justice, mercy, and faith. Though their physical offerings were both compliant and commendable, Jesus critiqued their matter based on motive and manner. The scribes and Pharisees were obviously known for 'marketing their morality'. Tangible offerings could be easily viewed and accounted for and allowed them to demonstrate explicitly their virtue. However, much of this was designed to be self-serving, since it did little to actually make a substantive difference in the lives of anyone other than themselves. Because the focus was on personal self rather than collective service, the leaders gave little consideration to what best benefitted their communities. Mercy, justice, and faith all support a dynamic and responsive concern for the wellbeing of diverse stakeholders and often also suggest that actions be evaluated based on fairness, equity, and the common good. These higher order criteria and their emphasis on engaging the external environment may alter perceptions and plans regarding what is truly right, righteous and required, and help organizations identify the balance between internal discretionary decisions and externally driven demands.

In order for this idealism to be replaced by pragmatism, we believe that the areas of underlying contention must be identified and examined. We do so with four issues, that based on our research tend to be significant sources of discord between Christian philosophy and strategic business thought. In the rest of the chapter we discuss these as a precursor to our efforts to systematically address them in plausible ways,

Interruption: Not only must Christian leadership be willing and able to question or disrupt status quo thinking and behavior, especially when these are perceived as immoral, but Christian leaders must also empower others to do the same when necessary. The conceptualization of Jesus as a revolutionary isn't necessarily novel, but positioning him as vehemently opposed to the status quo has been elevated to coincide with our preoccupation with change. This has also become congruent with recent positions in Christian leadership research that call for a subordination of managerial egos while advocating for more employee dissension, particularly in areas of ethical concern. This seemingly maverick approach, especially from subordinates, may be more conducive to contemporary Christianity. Essentially it is better for employees to be challenging and perhaps even contentious, rather than being complacent and/or even complicit. We address the empowerment of employee as well as the structure and responsibility for leadership and employees in Chapter 3 in our discussion of subsidiarity with solidarity.

We are not attempting to deny or diminish Jesus's 'activist activities', however we posit that His words and actions against the establishment weren't necessarily directed at the system itself, but what it had become under the leaders of the day. This is perhaps best clearly shown in His assertion in Matthew 5:17–20 that "He didn't come to abolish the law but to fulfill it." Even more telling his is vehement affirmation of the law, but with a convicting challenge to uphold both the letter and the love of the law.

It is obvious that Jesus never instructed anyone to instigate and implement interruptive behavior. Any contention with/challenge to the system speaks to the subversion of the system's spirit. Jesus wanted followers to do *better than*, not different from the scribes. This message was essential in the first verses of Matthew 5, where Jesus preaches what is perceived as His most radical teachings, the Beatitudes. Yet Christ almost immediately quells this conception by confirming his appreciation and approval of the law. And interestingly, Christ and his followers also seemingly supported not just the religious system but also the institutional structures that facilitated the commerce and government of the day. This is demonstrated by Christ's instruction to Peter to "render unto Caesar the things are his" (Mark 12:17) and Paul's teaching to Timothy to "pray for those in government" (1st Timothy 2:2).

We should state here that although we use these as examples of Christianity working with rather than against established systems and structures, we do not believe that it requires blind servitude to the system. Christianity has been and will continue to be a conduit for change, even radical change, but we posit that this change, particularly in organizational settings, is best when using synergistic thought and when implemented alongside the organization's central strategy. We discuss the necessity of Christian leaders being able to synergize religious faith, diverse opinions and cultures, and the law in Chapter 6 in our discussion of synergy, and the level of support necessary for employee empowerment and synergy in Chapter 5.

Arguably, this 'ideal of interruption' has limited the acceptability and utility of concepts like ethics, social responsibility, and even spirituality itself. Academics, authors, and advocates have unfortunately often found themselves swimming upstream by attempting to sacrifice organizational strategy in the name of true spirituality. The fact that these moral/normative ways of doing business haven't taken center stage or catalyzed the kind of cataclysmic change envisioned is potentially a cautionary tale to those like us who seek a new, more effective way to marry strategy and spirituality. Indeed, a significant impetus for this book came from our desire to position Christian leadership at the forefront of conventional strategic wisdom and to use it to inform rather than interrupt why and how organizations conduct effective business.

Identity: Christian workspaces are often unashamedly ready to tout their openness to employees, intimately integrating faith and functionality in their daily practices. Instead of individuals being circumspect and conservative in showcasing their identity, this call to preach and practice their beliefs within their organizational roles offers a distinct opportunity to pursue godly service, even in secular service.

Beyond the moral impetus for such a Christian imprint is the argued personal and organizational benefits that are likely to be derived from support of a Christian identity. While scant, there is empirical research specifically addressing these benefits. Specifically, there is research to support employees' value for ethics and social responsibility[6], purpose and personal development[7], as well as meaningfulness.[8]

However, what is potentially a win-win can become potentially troublesome if there is perceived incongruence between employee desires and organization/operational demands. If there is no conflict, then workers are more likely to be more committed to both their tasks as well their organizations. However, inconsistency may leave individuals construing their responsibilities as chores that are actually inhibiting and not invoking their calling from God.

This disenchantment may jeopardize meaningfulness, a key construct mediating the relationship between corporate social responsibility and employee attitude. If this sense of calling and purpose hinges on their expectations regarding the 'goodness' of the organization, even the most ethical, socially responsible, and/or Christian-like organizations may leave spiritually ambitious employees with a lack of focus, framework, and even faith.

Jesus himself dealt with the misconception/misinterpretation of earthly service to God. His consistent participation in what others saw as the trivial and menial things of life often left Him at odds with His critics as well as His followers. He constantly reminded them that true Christianity and Christian calling was solely based on servanthood, and that sacrifice and being faithful in and with small things are the precursors to God trusting us with weightier matters. (Matthew 20:28; Luke 16: 10–14).

This premise of grind over grandeur can be as unappealing to contemporary workers as it was to the religious hierarchy, disciples, and apostles in the bible. And this need to divorce the spiritual from the secular, or demote the latter to the former may make spirituality in the workplace more of a liability than a benefit. One of the primary purposes for us to develop this model was to address the question we asked in Chapter 1: How can I be an effective Christian and a capitalist simultaneously? We believe our model provides the framework to integrate one's Christian identity with his or her secular vocation in a way that is strategic and operational.

Instrumentality: This challenge deals specifically with the problematic nature of materialism. As Christians, we agree that strategy solely focused on profit and ignoring religious and spiritual principles is worrisome. There has been much

---

[6] Case, P., & Gosling, J. (2010). The spiritual organization: Critical reflections on the instrumentality of workplace spirituality. *Journal of Management, spirituality and Religion, 7*(4), 257–282. Turban, D. B., & Cable, D. M. (2003). Firm reputation and applicant pool characteristics. *Journal of Organizational Behavior, 24*(6), 733–751. Turban, D. B., & Greening, D. W. (1997). Corporate social performance and organizational attractiveness to prospective employees. *Academy of Management Journal, 40*(3), 658–672.

[7] Richardson, B. (2016). Chick-fil-A restaurants respond to Orlando massacre with free food at blood drives. *The Washington Times.*.

[8] Rupp D. E., Ganapathi J., Aguilera R.V., & Williams C. A. (2006). Employee reactions to corporate social responsibility: an organizational justice framework. *Journal of Organizational Behavior, 27*(4), 537–543.

written about money and materialism and its implications to Christianity, especially in the for-profit environment. Additionally, we address the Christian relationship with wealth in Chapter 4 in our discussion on stewardship. We find it unnecessary and even counter-productive to rehash much either as supporting material or as provokers of debate. Instead, we contend that any attempt, even a virtuous one, to link the subordination or sacrifice of financial success with workplace spirituality undermines the generalizability and acceptability of this construct in the workplace. Much like normative/altruistic CSR has found little traction or currency, we posit that the instrumentality of spirituality is not its scar but its true salience and salability.

Past attempts to mitigate or even moralize money have made topics like marketplace ministry more spiritually palatable, however they sorely undervalue the strategic merit of Christ-like approach to work and leadership. A strategic approach is fundamentally built on the precept of shared value and mutual benefit between firm and society.[9] The impersonality of such an orientation affords it a relative practicality and objectivity that are to some extent absent from a purely theological approach. To pursue God's glory is indeed biblical and important in the life of all Christians but this pursuit does not provide measures of productivity and performance which are necessary for strategic leadership.

In our approach we leverage the instrumentality of materialism in Christianity. We posit that Capitalism can and should be influenced by a compassion and care that can only be achieved through adopting a Christ-like strategic approach. But this approach must be balanced and incorporate a pragmatism that is clearly based in Jesus's perspective on money and economic systems. We thus make the bold assertions that instrumentality is critical to not just strategy, but strategy based on Christian principles, and that attempts to downplay or demonize its inclusion violate both business and the bible.

Internalization: Comparable and coinciding questions accompanying instrumentality include: what should motivate and govern/influence organizational behavior; and relatedly, should external forces and trends matter to firms that adopt a Christ-like approach. It could be argued that leaders use conduct codes and benchmarks as public relations tools. Instrumental and auditing approaches, both external and internal are easily manipulated and connived for unmerited gain. Of course, any strategic model is predicated on interpreting and responding effectively to the interest of diverse stakeholders, but does such an approach instigate compromise of Christian principles, priorities, and practices?

Organizations may be vehement and forceful in disavowing external shifts that seem unbiblical. And while these stances can accrue strong reputational capital, especially from ardent supports, they may also simultaneously and inadvertently isolate others that believe similarly, but uniquely. Chick-fil-A's view on homo-

---

[9] Porter, M. E., & Kramer, M. R. (2002). The competitive advantage of corporate philanthropy. *Harvard Business Review, 80*(12), 56–68.

sexuality and Hobby Lobby's stance on contraception are two relatively contemporary cases where fundamentalism clashed with freedom of choice and created uncertainty for both customers as well as the companies.

Remaining faithful while flexible is challenging but not novel. Early Christianity faced multiple instances where believers from different backgrounds had to reconcile varied circumstances and customs to help the embryonic movement to evolve and stay relevant. Paul, the self-confessed Jew of all Jews, was ironically the one who was a chief flag bearer. In Galatians 3:28 he stated that "there is neither Jew nor Gentile, neither slave nor free, nor is there male and female, for you are all one in Christ Jesus." He ascribed so strongly to this that he was willing to part ways with Peter over his (Peter's) unwavering support for Jewish custom.

As illustrated in this instance, defiance, especially 'doctrinal defiance' usually ignites deep division. The system turns inwardly and may fail to acknowledge the legitimate and diverse interest of the entirety of their stakeholder community. These interests typically show themselves through institutional and market forces and resistance to these may not only alienate those already with the firm, but also exclude permanently new talent or markets the organization wishes to reach.

Jesus himself left no doubt that His kingdom would look different from the traditionalist notion of the righteous. It would include those that had been ostracized and ignored because of their differences. His ministry and those of His subsequent church was to be representative of all society. Thus a social agenda is not only strategic but also sanctified, requiring firms to work synergistically with the external environment to fulfill heavenly as well as earthly objectives.

We believe the model we present will allow for idealism to be replaced by pragmatism. The principles of subsidiarity with solidarity, stewardship, support and empowerment, and synergy are presented to plausibly and systematically address the areas of underlying contention between Christian philosophy and strategic business thought examined above. In the rest of the book we present strategy in His image.

CHAPTER 3

SUBSIDIARITY WITH SOLIDARITY

...what seems necessary is a feasible approach that protects the power of the individual while simultaneously fostering coherence among all members in the organizational structure. For this, we turn to the concept of subsidiarity.

We believe that followership should never be a passive response to a dictatorial demand, especially in circumstances where leaders fail to uphold their vested mandate to their organization as well as to general society. Christian leadership must be willing and able to question or disrupt status quo thinking and behavior, especially when these are perceived as immoral, and the idea of independent thought and empowerment has shown to be effective in the context of contemporary management. Yet, as we have previously argued, there is a prevailing 'danger' that this spirit of independence and interruption might unduly/unintentionally create within an organization a climate of both subversion and suspicion between employees and their bosses. Workers emboldened to 'fight the good fight of faith' might unnecessarily undermine or even usurp established leadership, in an effort to uphold their notion of righteousness.

Therefore, what seems necessary is a feasible approach that protects the power of the individual, while simultaneously fostering coherence among all members

Strategy in His Image: Supporting and Sustaining Organizational Strategy
From a Christian Perspective, pages 19–26.
Copyright © 2023 by Information Age Publishing
www.infoagepub.com
19

in the organizational structure. For this, we turn to the concept of subsidiarity. Subsidiarity comes from the Catholic social tradition and refers to those in authority providing support rather than directing lesser communities and respecting the capacity of those receiving assistance, as creations of God, made in His image and gifted by God with free will and reason. This assumption is based in Genesis 1:27 So God created man in His own image; in the image of God He created him; male and female He created them (NKJV). The principles that underlie subsidiarity are generally viewed in what we'll call three buckets. First, respect for human freedom and dignity expressed the ability of all individuals, regardless of status, to make decisions and conduct business. Second, consideration of diversity where the importance of unity is understood but not enforced to the degree it prevents the development of natural diversity. Finally contributing to the common good where all involved, at all levels, must do all they can to reach fulfillment and collective goals.[1]

All of God's creation has a role and responsibility to fill, whether in authority or not, and those in authority have the additional responsibility to provide support and guidance without undue interference. This responsibility is significantly increased as individuals move up in authority. This is not necessarily the case because increased authority makes one more sinful, but because the decisions made at higher levels of authority can, and usually do, cause greater harm.[2] History is paved with harmful decisions, made by good people with good intentions. This type of order where every role, no matter how minor, is important to the whole and should be treated with dignity is what Paul seems to suggest to the church at Corinth in 1 Corinthians 12:12–27.

> [12] For as the body is one and has many members, but all the members of that one body, being many, are one body, so also *is* Christ. [13] For by one Spirit we were all baptized into one body—whether Jews or Greeks, whether slaves or free—and have all been made to drink [a]into one Spirit. [14] For in fact the body is not one member but many.
>
> [15] If the foot should say, "Because I am not a hand, I am not of the body," is it therefore not of the body? [16] And if the ear should say, "Because I am not an eye, I am not of the body," is it therefore not of the body? [17] If the whole body *were* an eye, where *would be* the hearing? If the whole *were* hearing, where *would be* the smelling? [18] But now God has set the members, each one of them, in the body just as He pleased. [19] And if they were all one member, where *would* the body *be?* [20] But now indeed *there are* many members, yet one body. [21] And the eye cannot say to the hand, "I have no need of you"; nor again the head to the feet, "I have no need of you." [22] No, much rather, those members of the body which seem to be weaker are necessary. [23] And those *members* of the body which we think to be less honorable, on these we

---

[1] Mele D., (2005) Exploring the principle of subsidiarity in organizational forms. *Journal of Business Ethics, 60,* 293–305.

[2] McIlroy, D. (2003). Subsidiarity and sphere sovereignty: Christian reflections on the size, shape and scope of government. *Law Justice The Christian Law Review, 151,* 111–136.

bestow greater honor; and our unpresentable *parts* have greater modesty, [24] but our presentable *parts* have no need. But God composed the body, having given greater honor to that *part* which lacks it, [25] that there should be no schism in the body, but *that* the members should have the same care for one another. [26] And if one member suffers, all the members suffer with *it;* or if one member is honored, all the members rejoice with *it.* [27] Now you are the body of Christ, and members individually. (NKJV)

In this illustration using the parts of the body, Paul suggests everyone in the body of Christ has roles and responsibilities to the body composed by God. God is the ultimate authority, and how God uses his authority is dependent on the lens in which one views the nature of God and the free will of man.

Subsidiarity seems to model the moderate/openness view, and possibly the progressive/process view of the relationship between God and humankind, however, we see subsidiarity as most consistent with open theology. Moderate and progressive theology, both view God by varying degrees as respectful of the decisions of man, and see man as a partner in history. As stated in chapter one, in the progressive view, man's actions and God's actions appear to be one and the same, and in the open view man's actions have a direct effect on God's actions and the execution of God's plan. In the open view Pinnock describes this partner relationship as one that God accepts seriously, allowing man the opportunity to participate in the shaping of one's own future and destiny generated by an ongoing interaction with God.[3] In addition to a respectful partnership, subsidiarity requires the authority to intervene to encourage, stimulate, regulate, supplement, and complement.[4] In the openness model God limits himself, but is genuinely involved in human history, taking actions to help direct man toward His goals of overcoming sin and loving relationships.[5] This suggests more intervention than progressive theology would allow.

Other intriguing questions arise when examining subsidiarity through a progressive lens: Who is the authority? What is the nature of the relationship? Pinnock et al states, "Progressive theology ranges from antirealism where God is merely our religious discourse or lifestyle to process theology where God is ontologically dependent on the world."[6] Using these definitions, with antirealism there is no relationship, and with process theology there is a relationship. Yet God is ontologically dependent on mankind, so He has no authority other than what mankind decides. Additionally, they suggest using the Tillich's understanding of God, "God can have no external relationship with creatures. To think of having personal relations with God or being his partner in action is impossible if God is

---

[3] Pinnock, C., (2001). *Most moved mover: A theology of God's openness* (p.57). Backer Academic.

[4] Van Til, K. A. (2008). Subsidiarity and sphere-sovereignty: A match made in . . . ? *Theological Studies; 69*(3), 610–636.

[5] Pinnock, C., Rice, R., Sanders, J., Hasker, W., & Basinger, D., (1994) *The openness of God A biblical challenge to the traditional understanding of God* (pp. 35–38). InterVarsity Press.

[6] Ibid, 92.

Being-Itself,..."[7] Subsidiarity requires clear lines of authority and a respectful relationship between those in authority and the communities in which they have authority. While it may be possible to execute subsidiarity through a progressive lens, fundamental questions, questions that we lack sufficient knowledge of progressive theology to attempt to answer, with any degree of confidence, would need to be answered. Subsidiarity would be a difficult fit viewed through a conservative lens. Through the conservative lens God directly controls and directs history to His will. The level of control exerted by God viewed through a conservative lens is inconsistent with subsidiarity.

Subsidiarity, in an organizational context, can be defined as a principle of decentralization whereby operational involvement and decision-making are accomplished by the organizational unit with greatest immediacy, familiarity and/or competency with the subject matter.[8] This diffusion of responsibility then positions the system's centralized authority as a subsidiary, acting as a complementing entity rather than a directorial presence, thereby supporting the diffusion of work throughout the entire system.[9] To illustrate subsidiarity in an organizational context, ethicist Domenec Mele presents a case study of a nonprofit mutual insurance company that works with the Spanish social security system handling industrial accidents and occupational diseases called Fremap.[10]

In the Fremap case employees participated in a process to identify the company's values. Through this process they identified two guiding principles: ethics and quality. The key here is that the ethics principle included the idea of the person at the center of social relationships. It was recognized by the company's CEO that there was a gap between the identified shared values and the structure of the organization due to its strict bureaucracy, high degree of specialization, and highly defined departments and job categories. To address this gap the company went to a more decentralized structure and the concept of an integral agent was introduced, where a single employee would be able to address all of a customer's problems.[11]

Fremap's new decentralized structure and reorganization of job categories aligning with the identified values was highly consistent with the guiding principles of subsidiarity. First, respect for human freedom and dignity was expressed in the identified values. Additionally, the ability of all individuals, regardless of status, to make decisions and conduct business was shown in the process to identify those values, as well as the responsibilities given to the integral agents. The rede-

---

[7] Ibid, 92.

[8] Daly, L. (2009). *God's economy: Faith-based initiatives and the caring state*. University of Chicago Press.

[9] Byron, W. J. (2006). *The power of principles: Ethics for the new corporate culture*. Orbis Books. Handy, C. B. (1994). *The age of paradox*. Harvard Business School Press.

[10] Mele D. (2005). Exploring the principle of subsidiarity in organizational forms. *Journal of Business Ethics, 60*, 293–305.

[11] Ibid. 296–296.

signed job would prevent upper levels of the company from doing tasks that could be done at lower levels. Second, giving agents the freedom to act independently to promote diversity of thought in engaging clients was balanced by each agent also being part of a team. The decentralized structure, reducing bureaucracy, and job design for the integral agent analogized the importance of unity or teamwork, while allowing for the development of natural diversity. Finally, included was contributing to the common good where all involved, at all levels, was required to do all they could to reach fulfillment and collective goals.

Subsidiarity promotes and prioritizes the value of organizational members, not just as objective contributors to economic output, but as gifted human beings with talents and pursuits far greater than their professional obligations.[12] It advocates for decentralization, but not through subordination or supplementation.[13] Instead, it urges leaders to identify, encourage, cultivate, and leverage the uniqueness of its charges, to benefit both employee and firm, independently, but also interdependently.[14] As with open theology's relationship between God and humankind, subsidiarity embraces a relationship between leadership and subordinates, where subordinates are allowed a 'constructive' level of individualism and self-authorship. Also, as with God's decision to create a world with free beings, it also recognizes that allowing independent thought and action can be a risky proposition, if not managed effectively and intimately.[15]

To avert or mitigate this risk, Naughton et al. introduced the concept of solidarity, defined as the "unity of a common good."[16] They argue poignantly that solidarity is a necessary complement to subsidiarity, and discuss how the latter without the former can lead to the troublesome issues. For example, they suggest that an approach that focuses on self rather than system (subsidiarity without solidarity) is likely to motivate "employees who are isolated from the market and the larger community." This preoccupation with self-reference, they further argue, may shift consideration away from collective obligations to individual rights, thereby discouraging shared identity and ultimately, the common good rather than "undisciplined empowerment."[17] This approach, we propose will foster individ-

[12] Alford, H. J., & Naughton, M. (2001). Managing as If Faith Mattered: Christian Social Principles in the Modern Organization. Notre Dame: University of Notre Dame

[13] Drucker, P.F. (2006). Classic Drucker: Essential Wisdom of Peter Drucker from the Pages of Harvard Business Review. Boston: Harvard Business Review Book.
Naughton, M., Buckeye, J., Goodpaster, K., & Maines T.D. (2015). Respect in Action: Applying Subsidiarity in Business. St Thomas University: UNIAPAC
Handy, C. B. (1994). *The Age of Paradox*. Boston, MA: Harvard Business School Press.

[14] Chamberlain, G. L., & Dickins, D. (2004). The evolution of business as a Christian calling. *Review of Business, Special Issue: Catholic Social Thought and Management Education, 25*(1), 27–36.
Drucker, P. F., & Collins. J. C. (2008). *The five most important questions you will ever ask about your organization*. Leader to Leader Institute.

[15] Naughton, M., et al. (2015). *Respect in action: Applying subsidiarity in business*. St Thomas University: UNIAPAC

[16] Ibid. 27.

[17] Ibid. 28.

ual employee engagement and discretion, but through the channels of a coherent commitment to a common cause.

The challenge for the Christian business leader in a multicultural and diverse environment is defining the common cause that meets his responsibility, as God's partner and at the same time, is viable for Christians and non-Christians. For organizations to thrive and evolve, the organizational identity is equally as important as the individual identities of its employees. The common cause, which we define as the organizational mission must be one everyone can celebrate, that promotes a set of common values and experiences everyone, Christian and Non-Christian, can share. This means developing an organizational environment that is open to and not just tolerant of individual cultures and beliefs, so that all their people can develop and grow personally and professionally. While developing an environment open to individual cultures and beliefs, there must be a commitment to the organizational mission and respect for the organizational culture. It must be emphasized that the commitment is to the organization's mission and not to its culture. Organizational culture is very important, but all cultures evolve and change, including corporate cultures. It is impossible to have a static organizational culture and at the same time be open to diverse cultures and differences. Just as American culture has evolved, as it has assimilated cultural aspects of all that have come to America, the same thing will necessarily happen to corporate cultures. We also must remember according to subsidiarity, all of God's creation has a role and responsibility. While it's leadership's role to develop an organization's culture, it's also employees' responsibility, either to identify organizations with cultures consistent with themselves or to adjust to cultures in cases where there is a fit with the mission. The challenge for leadership is to systemically reinforce the mission and values of its organization to provide guidance for the evolution of the organizational culture.

The organization's mission, however, is foundational, with minimal or no change at all. While leadership's job is to reinforce the mission and values of its organization, it's the mission that provides guidance to the leader as well as the employees and other stakeholders. A commitment to a mission consistent with God's word, for example, meeting the needs of man, Matthew 25:31–46, gives Christians the assurance that they are holding up their end of the partnership with God in their secular life. Concurrently, commitment to this mission gives non-Christians purpose and motivation in their work life. We believe that a commitment to a biblically based organizational mission can provide the solidarity necessary to make subsidiarity an effective strategy for leading people to reach organizational goals while fulfilling their responsibility as God's partner.

Because free willed imperfect people will hold the commitment to an organizational mission, even one based on biblical principles, the outcome can be anything from misuse due to an unintentional lack of focus or misinterpretation, to misuse due to intentional deceit or manipulation. The latter is simply evil that is beyond the scope of our model. However, to prevent the former is why we argue that all the principles identified in our model interact with each other and need to be reinforced through simultaneous engagement. Leaders must be intentional about all these principles individually as well as collectively. In this case, because commitment to the organization's mission is important, we must be clear on the role of profitability and wealth building as they are essential to operating in a capitalist economy, yet they can be so easily misused or become the primary focus. The accumulation of excess monetary wealth for the sake of accumulation could never be a legitimate pursuit for a Christian business leader, however the accumulation of resources to sustain an organization that meets the needs of a community, provides employment and development opportunities for its people, and provides a stable tax base is a legitimate aim for a Christian business leader. The paradox lies in the understanding that the accumulation of wealth is not necessarily bad and can be good, but concurrently material wealth is very seductive and extremely tempting. Therefore, Christians need guiding principles to build and use wealth while avoiding the tempting desire of the accumulation of wealth for wealth's sake, or the power and prestige that comes with wealth. The principle of stewardship (the focus of chapter 4) deals specifically with the role of financial gain. It is the simultaneous engagement between subsidiarity and solidarity along with stewardship that gives the Christian leader the ability to exercise his faith and meet his organizational responsibility.

In Paul's illustration in 1 Corinthians, 12: 12–27, he vividly notes, congruent subsidiarity, that all parts have independent, functional value and discounts any notion of superiority among these parts. However, importantly, he maintains the idea of subsidiarity and solidarity throughout by reminding his readers of the importance and primacy of support and unity. Theological scholars suggest Paul's use of oneness could be allocated for social as well as theological purposes.[18] We argue that this oneness should be allocated for organizational purposes also in the form of commitment to organizational mission. According to the Gospel of John, this idea of unity is echoed by Jesus himself in his pleas to heaven that all his disciples and followers "may be one as I and the father are one." (Bible, John 17: 21). Theologian Gert Breed in his article examining the use of the word daikon in the Bible puts it this way.

> The diakonos of Jesus is therefore also an agent who communicates the words of Christ—which are the Words of the Father—to others. The aim of the communication is that the others should accept the words in faith and believe them and that they would be drawn to Christ by the words. Whoever believes and follows Jesus serves him, and whoever serves Jesus will be with him. It is clear from John 15 and 17 that being with Jesus entails that believers become part of the community between the Father and the Son and that believers are one with each other. When this unity

---

[18] Byers, A. (2016). The one body of the Shema in 1 Corinthians: An Ecclesiology of Christological Monotheism. *New Testament Studies: Cambridge, 62*, 517–532.

becomes visible, it makes the testimony of the believers effective so that others will also come to the faith (see 17:20–23; Kysar 2001:372)."[19]

The sometimes competing concepts of unity and individuality are clearly critical to organizational and theological contexts. The concept of subsidiarity with solidarity provides the framework to strike the necessary balance to create the type of unity that becomes visible in order to make the testimony of believers or the work of employees effective in reaching their goals.

---

[19] Breed, G., (2014). The meaning of the diakon word group in John 12:26 applied to the ministry in congregations. *Verbum et Ecclesi, 35*, 1–8.

CHAPTER 4

STEWARDSHIP

Inherently, one cannot practice true stewardship without to some extent adopting a selfless and servanthood orientation. But rather than conflicting with the precept of profit maximization, we argue that effective stewardship advocates the marriage of morality and money.

In what is colloquially described as the Parable of the Talents, Jesus discusses the attitude and approach of three servants to the management of their master's wealth.

[14] "For *the kingdom of heaven is* like a man traveling to a far country, *who* called his own servants and delivered his goods to them. [15] And to one he gave five talents, to another two, and to another one, to each according to his own ability; and immediately he went on a journey. [16] Then he who had received the five talents went and traded with them, and made another five talents. [17] And likewise he who *had received* two gained two more also. [18] But he who had received one went and dug in the ground, and hid his lord's money. [19] After a long time the lord of those servants came and settled accounts with them. [20] "So he who had received five talents came and brought five other talents, saying, 'Lord, you delivered to me five talents; look, I have gained five more talents besides them.' [21] His lord said to him, 'Well *done, good and faithful servant;* you were faithful over a few things, I will make you ruler over many things. Enter into the joy of your lord.' [22] He also who had received two

Strategy in His Image: Supporting and Sustaining Organizational Strategy
From a Christian Perspective, pages 27–32.
Copyright © 2023 by Information Age Publishing
www.infoagepub.com

talents came and said, 'Lord, you delivered to me two talents; look, I have gained two more talents besides them.' [23] His lord said to him, 'Well *done,* good and faithful servant; you have been faithful over a few things, I will make you ruler over many things. Enter into the joy of your lord.'

[24] "Then he who had received the one talent came and said, 'Lord, I knew you to be a hard man, reaping where you have not sown, and gathering where you have not scattered seed. [25] And I was afraid, and went and hid your talent in the ground. Look, *there* you have *what is* yours.' [26] "But his lord answered and said to him, 'You wicked and lazy servant, you knew that I reap where I have not sown, and gather where I have not scattered seed. [27] So you ought to have deposited my money with the bankers, and at my coming I would have received back my own with interest. [28] So take the talent from him, and give *it* to him who has ten talents. [29] 'For to everyone who has, more will be given, and he will have abundance; but from him who does not have, even what he has will be taken away. [30] And cast the unprofitable servant into the outer darkness. There will be weeping and gnashing of teeth.' (NKJV)

Two servants were lauded for their willingness and ability to grow their initial investment while the other was heavily chided for both his risk aversion and wastefulness of opportunity. Through this story, Jesus introduces his audience to the concept of stewardship, i.e. the ethic of responsibility. The dictionary definition of stewardship is "the careful and responsible management of something entrusted to one's care." The dictionary definition and the parable of the talents suggest stewardship requires individuals to view resources and opportunities as charges, requiring dutiful management and preservation, to promote sustainability and social well-being. Stewardship therefore encourages other-centricity, but via the prudent use and growth of material assets. Biblically, this concept of stewardship seems to go back as far as creation when God gave human kind the responsibility to exercise dominion over all of creation.

[26] Then God said, "Let Us make man in Our image, according to Our likeness; let them have dominion over the fish of the sea, over the birds of the air, and over the cattle, over all the earth and over every creeping thing that creeps on the earth." [27] So God created man in His *own* image; in the image of God He created him; male and female He created them. [28] Then God blessed them, and God said to them, "Be fruitful and multiply; fill the earth and subdue it; have dominion over the fish of the sea, over the birds of the air, and over every living thing that moves on the earth." (NKJV)

The responsibilities inherent with stewardship make it not only consistent with, but foundational to the progressive/process and moderate/open views of God. For process theology, because God is constricted by man as God is ontologically dependent on the world it could be argued that humankind's stewardship is the ultimate expression of God. For openness theology, because God chose to give man free will in order to have a loving relationship where one can choose to accept or reject God making the execution of his will to some degree dependent on the actions of man, the execution of God's will is directly affected by mankind's stewardship of God's blessings.

As stated previously, stewardship deals specifically with the management and growth of material assets. Given that, we must deal specifically with the relationship between Christianity and wealth. Robert Kennedy, in his examination of business and wealth creation in the context of Christian Social Thought posits that scriptures differentiate between wealth as an excess of material goods at the expense or in opposition to the poor, and as a life ambition, versus abundance and prosperity. The wealthy, as a particular segment of the society, or the "rich man" is usually portrayed as unjust, while communities and individuals are usually blessed by God with abundance and prosperity.[1] In his development of a biblical theology of stewardship, Blomberg does a significant analysis of the biblical text examining the triad of God, mankind, and wealth.[2] Blomberg presents biblical evidence of the goodness of wealth from the old and the new testaments. In the Deuteronomic Covenant in Leviticus 26:3–13 God promises lush land and harvests, peace, numerical growth, and that He will provide for them abundantly should they follow his commandments.[3] Within Proverbial Wisdom Psalm 25:13 assures those that fear the Lord will spend their days in prosperity and their descendants will inherit the land.[4] As for Prophetic Pronouncements, Blomberg points to the messianic banquet in Isaiah 25:6–8 where God provides a feast of rich food, and the best aged wine.[5] In the new testament Blomberg speaks to the Gospels where Jesus accepted invitations to banquet with the well off and Jesus allowed Mary of Bethany to anoint him with contents of a bottle worth a year's wages.[6] Finally he speaks to the well to do that were believers in the early church, and Paul's perspective that those that have excess must give generously, but Paul does not command to give up everything but the basics for life.[7] Even when Kennedy's examination speaks of the "rich man," Bloomberg's analysis suggests these are spiritual issues manifested in economic self-centeredness, which discloses the lack of a relationship with God.[8]

Similarly, Bloomberg provides an equally detailed biblical examination from Genesis to Revelations on the seductive nature of wealth and how easily without proper perspective, material possessions lead to sin.[9] We'd argue that there is a negative or inverse correlation between spiritual and material wealth or the lack thereof, however there is no causal effect. Bloomberg's extensive study confirms

---

[1] Kennedy, R. (2012). *The good that business does* (pp. 63–65). Acton Institute.
[2] Blomberg, C. L. (2013). *Christians in an age of wealth: A biblical theology of stewardship.* Zondervan.
[3] Ibid. 44–45.
[4] Ibid. 48.
[5] Ibid. 51.
[6] Ibid. 55.
[7] Ibid. 58.
[8] Ibid. 159–161.
[9] Ibid. 67–95.

for us our belief that biblically, wealth is not necessarily good or bad, but that wealth is an important part of the biblical story and Christian tradition. Therefore, particularly from the openness theological perspective, for effective stewardship Christian business leaders have a responsibility to think about and manage wealth in ways that are consistent with the responsibility of being God's partner in history.

Because business organizations have a bigger role in the modern economy for the creation of wealth compared to the consumption of it and the execution of God's will being at a minimum, somewhat dependent on the actions of mankind, stewardship requires Christian organizational leaders to ensure the sustainability of their organizations and that the wealth generated by their organizations contribute to the prosperity of all. This view on the relationship between Christian thought and Christian business responsibility is summed up nicely by Pope Pius XI: "Expending larger incomes so that opportunity for gainful work may be abundant should be considered an outstanding exemplification of the virtue of munificence and one particularly suited to the needs of the times."[10]

When addressing what could be competing priorities like other-centricity and growth of material assets, organizational leaders need frameworks to strike a proper balance. Some scholars dictate that profit be subordinate to perceived social purposes.[11] In fact, their appeal to 'think theologically not materially' seemingly presumes that true Christianity and pure Capitalism, at least cognitively, cannot be pursued simultaneously. We contend this confluence is not necessarily incorrect. Inherently, one cannot practice true stewardship without to some extent adopting a selfless and servanthood orientation. But rather than conflicting with the precept of profit maximization, we argue that effective stewardship advocates the marriage of morality and money. Independently, each view suffers from incompleteness and ignorance. Money, sans morality, engenders avarice that would never be acceptable to Christians or any people of faith. However, morality without explicit consideration of profit can be equally dangerous, by undermining economic sustainability.[12]

Theoretically and empirically, a viable integration of both has proven to be both palatable and prescriptive.[13] The concept of mutually matching firm strengths with community service has bridged any gaps or contradictions among profit, people, and planet.[14] Firms are also finding novel ways to coincide conventional

---

[10] Kennedy, R., (2012). *The good that business does* (p. 65). Acton Institute.

[11] Mabey, C., Conroy, M., Blakeley, K., & de Marco, S. (2016). Having burned the straw man of Christian spiritual leadership, what can we learn from Jesus about leading ethically? *Journal of Business Ethics.* doi:10.1007/s10551-016-3054-5

[12] Lantos, G. P. (2002). The ethicality of altruistic corporate social responsibility. *Journal of Consumer Marketing, 19*(3), 205–232.

[13] Orlitzky, M., Siegel, D. S., & Waldman, D. A. (2011). Strategic corporate social responsibility and environmental sustainability. *Business & Society, 50*(1), 6–27.

[14] Porter, M. E., & Kramer, M. R. (2002). The competitive advantage of corporate philanthropy. *Harvard Business Review, 80*(12), 56–68. Ricks Jr., J. M. (2005). An assessment of strategic corpo-

business goals with additional social support as attested to by 'Bottom of Pyramid' strategies and other such social entrepreneurship.[15] Consistent with this perspective, Hunt and Morgan in their presentation of comparative advantage theory as an alternative to neoclassical theory argue that firms operate to achieve superior financial performance under constrained self-interest and not profit or wealth maximization. They argue that "both consumers and managers are constrained in their self-interest seeking by considerations of what is right, proper, ethical, moral, or appropriate.[16] Many managers avoid cheating and exploiting customers not only for the fear of being caught, but for many managers, Christian managers particularly; they also avoid these behaviors because they are simply wrong.

Critics of capitalism and corporations specifically, frequently point to "excessive profits" as the sin of capitalists, however Hunt and Morgan correctly argue profits and returns on investments are relative to competitors and will vary between firms, industries, and nations. Firms' goals are usually not to get the maximum profit possible, but to get the profit level necessary to beat competitors. It is also common for firms to have other goals such as market share which usually reduce profits for that time period. Additionally, according to the National Philanthropic Trust in 2019 corporations donated $20.05 billion dollars to charity.[17] Even if one argues that the dollar amount could or should be more, one cannot argue that taking $20 plus billion dollars from profit generating projects to give to charity is profit maximizing behavior.

We argue that the integration of the responsibility of Christian business leaders for the financial sustainability of their organizations and ensuring the resources they amass benefit all is strategically sensible and is also biblically based. The Parable of the Talents itself is a testament to Jesus's belief that material gain is not offensive, but potentially constructive, if managed and motivated appropriately. Paul, similarly, is not antagonistic towards wealth, but proposes that Christians should use these material gains philanthropically (Bible, 1 Timothy 6: 17–19). Eubank argues the commandment found in verse 14 in the Good Confession (1 Timothy 6: 11–14) is Almsgiving.[18] In order to follow this commandment there must be people with material means and a desire to give to the poor. Profitable organizations can organize capital to do great works for people in need. As we see how all the principles in the model interact, not only can organizations provide for those in need through stewardship, but they can also provide individual and collective purpose through the principle of subsidiarity with solidarity and syner-

---

rate philanthropy on perceptions of brand equity variables. *Journal of Consumer Marketing, 22*(3), 121–134.

[15] Prahalad, C. K. (2012). Bottom of the pyramid as a source of breakthrough innovations. *Journal of Product Innovation Management, 29*(1), 6–12.

[16] Hunt, S. D., & Morgan, R. M. (1995). The comparative advantage theory of competition. *The Journal of Marketing*, 1–15.

[17] https://www.nptrust.org/philanthropic-resources/charitable-giving-statistics/

[18] Eubank, N. (2012). Almsgiving is 'the commandment: A note on 1 Timothy 6.6–19. *New Testament Studies, 58*, 144–150.

gy, and they can provide professional development and enrichment of employees through support and empowerment. The interaction of these principles provides the Christian business leader a great deal of tools to help fulfill his or her role as God's partner in history through his or her secular life, and the considerable responsibility that comes along with it.

CHAPTER 5

SUPPORT AND EMPOWERMENT

Not only must Christian business leaders be able to engage with diverse populations, they must also create an environment where teams from diverse cultures and backgrounds can engage with each other, feel supported, and be a part of the organizational mission. Just as Jesus identified and cultivated his disciples toward his ministry and ultimately to the great commission, business leaders must select and cultivate their teams toward the organizational mission.

Redefining work as a purposeful life choice is a defining characteristic of many spiritual approaches to leadership and business. Employees and their efforts should have greater meaning than the products and services they help deliver. The challenge for Christian leaders is creating this type of environment without creating either a closed organizational community or disenchanted, nomadic members. In other words, to lead an organization based on Christian principles where Christian and Non-Christians are supported and empowered; where a Christian leader can be true to their values and self-identity as a Christian and have a diverse and inclusive workforce. In his book Small Giants, Bo Burlingham provides an example of an organization, Reell Precision Manufacturing, that illustrates the operational

Strategy in His Image: Supporting and Sustaining Organizational Strategy
From a Christian Perspective, pages 33–38.
Copyright © 2023 by Information Age Publishing
www.infoagepub.com

challenges faced by firms attempting to be more 'Christian like,' by replacing the corporation with the church.[1] As Burlingham, discussing Reell notes:

> They instituted an optional weekly Bible class that employees could attend on company time, but they asked only that employees support the company's values, not the founders' religious beliefs, and they went out of their way to welcome employees of other faiths as well as nonbelievers. Nevertheless, Reell inevitably attracted a significant number of born-again employees, and they were not as sensitive as the partners to others who might not share their beliefs. When it appeared that the Bible-study meetings were creating divisions in the company rather than fostering unity and mutual commitment, they were canceled. (p 126)

At church we are in a space where we engage with other believers with very similar belief systems, in that everyone has not only accepted Christ, but also has accepted a doctrine, covenant, or articles of faith. Business leaders don't have this luxury. Business leaders not only have the fiduciary, but also the legal and moral responsibility to provide leadership to diverse teams. Not only must Christian business leaders be able to engage with diverse populations, they must also create an environment where teams from diverse cultures and backgrounds can engage with each other, feel supported, and be a part of the organizational mission. Just as Jesus identified and cultivated his disciples toward his ministry and ultimately to the great commission, business leaders must select and cultivate their teams toward the organizational mission. As with subsidiarity with solidarity, the organizational mission must be one everyone can celebrate and promote; a set of common values and experiences everyone Christian and Non-Christian can share.

When Jesus chose his disciples, he ignored the existing religious leaders. Instead, he admitted fishermen, tax collectors, doctors, and other ordinary secular people to further his mission on earth. Interestingly, Jesus's method of recruitment was less about enlistment and more about engagement. None of his followers initially were motivated by meeting the mandate of God but were drawn to and empowered by the man and the message. In the Gospels of Matthew 4:12–20 and Mark 1:14–20 Jesus was preaching the gospel and repentance when He called His first disciples and they followed Him. In Luke 5:1–10 Jesus was also preaching but He also fished with Peter, increasing his catch before calling him to follow.

Jesus's ability to empower his disciples is documented in John 21.[2] According to Hoehl (2008) John 21 provides a comprehensive case study of Jesus's use of empowerment to develop his disciples, Peter in particular, due to his leadership role and eventual martyrdom.[3] In the rehabilitation of Peter, John 21 addresses three contemporary areas of development; confidence and self-efficacy, values

---

[1] Burlingham, B. (2007). *Small giants. companies that choose to be great instead of big.* Penguin.

[2] Hoehl, S., (2008). Empowered by Jesus: A research proposal for an exploration of Jesus:" Empowerment approach in John 21: 1–25. *The Journal of Applied Christian Leadership; Berrien Springs,* 2, 6–18.

[3] Ibid. 16.

and beliefs, and work-related skills. Throughout the text, Jesus challenged the disciples' values and beliefs in everything from fishing methods to their love for him. Each time he provided support giving the disciples the opportunity for success, thereby increasing self-efficacy and confidence. Whether it was catching fish on the right side of the boat instead of the left or challenging Peter's love for Him three times, to reinstate him following his three denials, Jesus' challenges were used to develop the disciples for their shift in vocation from fishermen to ministers of the gospel.

We propose that much like Jesus, Christian business orientations should be careful to be supportive and empowering in their approach to 'catching' and cultivating employees as opposed to relying on pre-established selection criteria to bring in the "right" employees. This implies that organizations may provide access and opportunity for spiritual enlightenment and/or development but all attempts must be made to make these efforts inclusive as well as beneficial to the good of the organization. Christian business leaders should be mindful of protecting the integrity of the work environment from all subversive elements, especially those that confuse conversion and collegiality. To be supportive and empowering specifically to Christians, leaders must create an environment where conversion is neither required nor prevented and collegiality is required and accepted.

It is also important for Christian business leaders to understand that discipleship is a multilayered process, with varying commitments to ministry and secular occupations.[4] In his 1871 classic The Training of the Twelve, A.B. Bruce outlines the three stages Jesus's disciples progressed through, from believers and occasional companions, to uninterrupted attendance involving the entire or habitual abandonment of secular occupations, to a select band of followers trained for apostleship.[5] Modern day disciples working in or leading organizations will generally be in stage one or at best in the early period of stage two, meaning they will have significant secular work responsibilities not related to ministry. The environment and work tasks developed by Christian leaders should be on a continuum from one end, at the very least, not being in direct conflict with Christian principles to the other end of directly supporting biblically based Christian principles.

The interaction between support and empowerment and subsidiarity with solidarity is clear and important as both support and empowerment and subsidiarity with solidarity must be directed toward the organizational mission. As stated in chapter 3, the challenge for the Christian business leader in a multicultural and diverse environment is defining the common cause or organizational mission that at least does not conflict with, but preferably meets his responsibility as God's partner and, at the same time, is viable for Christian and non-Christian employees. As with stewardship, support and empowerment is consistent with and foundational to the progressive/process and moderate/open views of God. Our position

---

[4] Burce, A. B. (1871). *The training of the twelve.* The Jackson Institute.
[5] Ibid. 12.

is due to the fact that within these views God's relationship with human kind is a partnership to varying degrees, and the execution of His will is at least somewhat dependent on the actions of humans. The life of Christians is directly affected by all humans in our communities. The blessing of God's love as well as the Earth and all its natural resources are used by all of humanity, Christian and non-Christian alike. For Christians within organizations, our effectiveness and career development are affected by everyone in the organization, regardless of their faith or lack thereof. The same holds true for organizational effectiveness; it's affected by everyone. For organizations to evolve and thrive the organizational identity must be just as important as the individual identities of its employees. We argue that the defining construct of that organizational identity is the organization's mission. In addition to the mission being one everyone can celebrate, promote, and share, leadership must cultivate it by supporting and empowering their employees to achieve it. Therefore, along with the environment and work tasks, the mission must also fall on the afore mentioned continuum.

We think it is important here to clarify the continuum. When we state that the mission, environment, and work tasks should preferably directly support biblically based Christian principles, this does not mean the organization's mission should be evangelical. Organizationally it is the church's mission to evangelize sinners. The mission of business organizations is to bring products and services to the market place to meet the needs of the people where they operate. As we discussed in chapter one, in market driven economies like the United States, strategic-business decisions have major implications for an organization's profitability and sustainability as well as the access to goods and services for God's creation. In the vast majority of cases where we have a need, we have to buy something in the market place in order to meet it, therefore pricing and distribution decisions among others have a direct effect on the ability of people to access goods and services to meet their needs. An organization whose mission is to produce or distribute food for a particular market or even the world's population would be one supporting the biblically based Christian principle found in the description of the last judgement Matthew 25:31–46.

Specifically verse 35; for I was hungry and you gave Me food; I was thirsty and you gave Me drink; I was a stranger and you took Me in would support an organizational mission of a food manufacturer. Clearly it can be argued that the scripture says "you gave me" not that "you sold me." However, we argue that even a charity that gives food has to get it from a supplier and in the modern economy that starts with manufacturers. Strategic decisions affecting production cost, distribution, and use of slack resources at a company like Hormel has a direct effect on organizations like Second Harvesters or local churches to provide food at no cost to those in need.

We recognize the significant contribution a renewed spirituality based in Christian principles to the workplace can have on employee productivity and general well-being.[6] However, there is a substantial difference between employees viewing work as a purely secular vocation and perceiving it as a righteous role. As stated earlier, many disciples will have significant secular work responsibilities not related to ministry, but as identified on the other side of the continuum the mission, environment, and/or work tasks cannot be in direct conflict with Christian principles. In the Reell Precision Manufacturing case, Burlingham tells of a story involving a conflict between engineering and sales in the design of a display hinge ordered by a design firm. It was obvious that the hinge was designed for convenience store and trade show displays for cigarettes. The engineer did not want to do the design as a matter of conscious; sales argued that Reell was not selling cigarettes and the design would have a great deal of applications that could be sold to many other companies. Additionally, this was during a time where all employees except for those at the bottom of the pay scale were taking pay cuts to avoid layoffs. This impasse was presented to one of the co-CEOs, Bob Carlson, whose response was "It'll be interesting to see how you guys figure this out." The decision ultimately went up to a group that headed the business development group and they decided not to move forward with the project.[7] It is questionable if the development of the hinge presented a direct conflict of Christian principles, but it was clearly in violation of the conscious of the engineer and would be viewed as a conflict of Christian principles to some Christians. What Reell teaches us here is the importance of leadership empowering and supporting employees' issues of conscious.

We contend that many of the benefits and outcomes of workplace spirituality may be derived without firms and employees unequivocally embracing organizational activity as the pursuit of God's kingdom and that ironically, stressing calling vs. career may unduly impose pressure on workers to meet even greater expectations, thereby making work more burdensome and unfulfilling. Again, we turn to the Reell Precision Manufacturing case where over a decade they developed a Direction Statement. This statement preserved the values, management concepts, and ideals exposed by the company founders; acknowledging the company's Christian roots without the evangelistic tones of earlier documents. For example, it did speak of operating a business on Judeo-Christian values and creating harmony between work and our moral and ethical values. However, it did not mention offering employees "an opportunity to integrate Christian life with a career[8]." Reell is clearly on the right side of the continuum where their mission, environment, and work task directly support biblically based Christian principles and has over time learned to balance ministry and secular occupations.

---

[6] Case, P., & Gosling, J. (2010). The spiritual organization: Critical reflections on the instrumentality of workplace spirituality. *Journal of Management, spirituality and Religion, 7*(4), 257–282.

[7] Burlingham, B. (2007). *Small giants. Companies that choose to be great instead of big* (pp. 119–121). Penguin

[8] Ibid. 128.

Research has identified six imperatives that would make up an ideal organization. These include companies where individuality is nurtured, information is not suppressed or spun, the company adds value to the employee, the company stands for something meaningful, work is intrinsically rewarding, and no stupid rules[9]. As wonderful as these virtues may sound, a deeper dive could show how they could be counterproductive or even detrimental to an organization on their own. Something as meaningful as adding value to employees, if not executed in a proper business context could reduce value for customers and damage the organization in the long run. For example, an organization could continuously raise employee compensation. This would be a clear-cut way of adding value to employees. However, this could become quite problematic if it requires continuously raising prices to cover the cost. This, just as clearly would reduce value to consumers and eventually lead to pricing that is noncompetitive. While adding value to employees is a virtuous pursuit that should be undertaken, it must be done responsibly and in context. In other words, the business environment must act as a rudder to this and all of the six identified virtues. Similarly, in our model, like solidarity acts as a rudder to subsidiarity, workplace spirituality must be tempered with an explicit appreciation that employees are spiritual beings with vocational responsibilities. And while these two may be integrated and intertwined, organizations and employees must ensure that spirituality helps rather than hurts; it is not disruptive, distractive, or divisive. We posit that using the principles identified in our model and a commitment to mission that is at best consistent with God's word giving Christians the assurance that they are in partnership with God in their secular life or is at least neutral, providing both Christians and non-Christians purpose and motivation in their work life, will provide a framework for Christian business leaders to provide the supportive and empowering environment for individual, vocational, and spiritual growth as well as organizational success.

[9] Goffee, R., & Jones, G. (2013). Creating the best workplace on earth. *Harvard Business Review,* *91*(5), 98–106.

CHAPTER 6

SYNERGY

When leading a business enterprise, particularly a large diverse one, these interactions are amplified by time pressure, resource limitations, and demands from competing stakeholders. The concept of synergy is critical for Christian business leaders to manage these critical interactions while intentionally staying committed to their faith.

In his national best seller, Stephen Covey identifies synergy as the driver of the principle of creative cooperation. He defines synergy as the whole being greater than the sum of its parts and the relationship which the parts have to each other. It is that relationship or interaction between diverse people and concepts that creates the challenge Covey identifies as applying the principles of creative cooperation learned from nature to our social interactions.[1] We define synergy as the combination of people or concepts to create new alternatives, actions, and/or outputs. For teams of individuals to achieve synergy and its benefits, there must be a congruence of core values, purpose, beliefs, and actions.[2] In order for a diverse population to achieve this congruency, there must be an ideal all can focus on along with the requisite flexibility in implementation to allow for the diversity of ideas

---

[1]Covey, S. (1989). *The seven habits of highly effective people.* Simon & Schuster.

[2] Lawford, G. (2003). Beyond success: Achieving synergy in teamwork. *The Journal for Quality and Participation, 26*(3), 23–27.

---

to converge. This could be the most perplexing concept for churched Christians because it requires challenging the strict implementation of orthodoxy. In diverse populations with varying perspectives orthodoxy will necessarily be challenged and in some cases, as uncomfortable as it may be for some of us in the Christian community, Christian doctrine based on current longstanding biblical interpretations will not always hold. This is clearly demonstrated in the history of the Christian church and science.

John Dillenberger, in his book Protestant Thought and Natural Science, provides an in-depth analysis of the debates between theology and science and the issues that were critical to those involved in the debates.[3] As confident as we are today about our doctrines based on scripture, there were doctrines and beliefs held by some of the greatest Christian minds based on scripture that we know today were clearly wrong. Based on the literalistic interpretation of Isaiah 40:22, both Lactantius and Augustine considered it impossible for there to be people living on the opposite side of the earth because it would have been impossible for Adam's ancestors to cross the ocean.[4] By the mid sixteenth century it was widely known that the earth was round and explorers had crossed the ocean. While a strict literalistic interpretation of Isaiah 40:22 had to be abandoned, men of God at the time still had a clear picture of the universe that could be biblically defended. At the center of the universe was the immovable earth and hell was the greatest distance from the heavens, at the center of the earth. This view was more philosophical in nature. It was based on Aristotelian thought rather than biblical revelation or scientific knowledge, however it gave Christians a special status at the center of the universe. Additionally, it had some biblical support, like Joshua commanding the sun to stand still.[5] While this shift to modern day Christians may not seem significant, we must put ourselves in the shoes of Christians of the time. They believed based on the preaching and teaching of the Word of God that the earth was flat. Imagine the discomfort as they learned that what they clearly thought they understood according to God's word was wrong. We can almost imagine that the suggestion of a round antipode earth would have received a response similar to the response given to tough questions regarding theology as we understand it today: "God said it, I believe it, that settles it."

Today, not only do we know of the round antipode earth, we also know the Aristotelian model of the universe with the earth in the center is not correct. It is common knowledge that sixteenth century theologians rejected Copernicus. It wasn't until the work of Kepler and Galileo that there was clear scientific evidence of the Copernican position, and it was Newton that made the Copernican position scientifically indisputable.[6] This history provides a clear example of the degree that religion (faith), philosophy, and science (observable knowledge) in-

---

[3] Dillenberger, J. (1988). *Protestant thought and natural science*. The University of Notre Dame Press.
[4] Ibid. 21.
[5] Ibid. 22–23.
[6] Ibid. 27–28.

teract. Even though they did not operate in a spirit of creative cooperation, Covey suggests the public debates of theologians, philosophers, and scientists forced synergy among these differing perspectives, and as Covey predicted, a new more accurate understanding of the natural universe and scripture's place in it was created. The concept of synergy is critical for Christian business leaders to manage these critical interactions while intentionally staying committed to their faith.

It's not just in the understanding of natural phenomena where our faith interacts with philosophy and secular knowledge. Even more relevant to demonstrating the need for synergy is how these interactions influence culture and how we understand scripture. In her extremely thought provoking book *Unprotected Texts the Bible's Surprising Contradictions about Sex and Desire*, Jennifer Knust provides an in-depth study regarding what the bible says and does not say regarding sex and sexuality. Both Ruth as well as David and Bathsheba engaged in sexual activity outside the bonds of marriage and were blessed by God, not cursed.[7] Ruth was a Moabite, decedents of an industrious relationship between Lot—brother of Abraham—and one of his daughters. Israelites were instructed to avoid Moabites due to their worship of Baal. However, Ruth's commitment to care for her deceased husband's mother Naomi led the two women on a journey from Moab to Judah, where Ruth would eventually give birth to Obed, the grandfather of David.[8] Bathsheba's adulterous relationship with David did lead to the loss of her life and their son Absalom's, however David and Bathsheba continued the royal bloodline by conceiving King Solomon.[9] The patriarch Judah is the eponym of the kingdom of Judah and the land of Judea, and it was the line produced by Judah and Tamar, (his daughter-in-law he solicited as a prostitute[10]), not the line produced by him and his wife Shuah, that is of the bloodline of great kings of Israel and Jesus himself.

The purpose here is not to debate the morality of specific sexual activities or the punishment or lack thereof for these activities. What Knust provides are demonstrations to show our biblically based religious beliefs and doctrines are often based on the cultural norms of the time and don't always line up with scripture as clearly as we would like. This should provide the requisite humility necessary to achieve synergy. Knust's study shows us that like in the natural world, we Christians must operate with the interaction of faith, philosophy, and science. Christians in a diverse cultural world have to operate by synergizing religious faith, cultural interpretations, and behavioral observations. In business organizations Christian leaders must synergize religious faith, diverse opinions and cultures, and perhaps more importantly, the law. Jesus clearly acknowledged civil law in his life and its place in the world, most notably in Matthew 22:21 when he states,

---

[7] Knust, J. (2011). *Unprotected texts the bible's surprising contradictions about sex and desire.* HarperCollins Publishers.
[8] Ibid. 34–35.
[9] Ibid. 45.
[10] Ibid. 5.

"Render therefore to Caesar the things that are Caesar's, and to God the things that are God's."(NKJV). In John 19:11 Jesus acknowledges the power given to Pilate to enforce civil law is given by God; Jesus answered, "You could have no power at all against Me unless it had been given you from above. Therefore the one who delivered Me to you has the greater sin." (NKJV). Additionally, Paul in 1 Timothy 2:1-2 not only acknowledges the authority of government, but also asks that they be prayed for. Therefore I exhort first of all that supplications, prayers, intercessions, and giving of thanks be made for all men, for kings and all who are in authority, that we may lead a quiet and peaceable life in all godliness and reverence (NKJV).

For Christians leading business enterprises, particularly large diverse ones, these interactions between faith, observable knowledge, philosophy, culture, and the law are amplified by time pressure, resource limitations, and demands from competing stakeholders. It is important to note that synergy is critical for not only being open to diverse thoughts, beliefs, and opinions, but also to ensure our Christian perspective is maintained. The case of Chick-Fil-A's response to the Pulse nightclub shooting provides an examples of what we believe to be synergistic leadership.

In 2016, a 29-year-old man killed 49 people and wounded 53 more in a mass shooting at Pulse, a gay nightclub in Orlando, Florida. In the wake of this horrific attack, many business organizations were quick to offer to the victims and official responders both vocal support as well as tangible assistance. One such organization was Chick-Fil-A. The restaurant chain made and delivered food to those waiting in line to donate blood to victims as well as to medical and police officials working in the aftermath of the attacks.[11]

These actions were relatively conspicuous, considering that employees of the firm were working on a Sunday, a day that the organization has traditionally closed its doors in the commemoration of the 'Christian Sabbath.' Further, and perhaps more surprising, was that these actions were in response to violent events that targeted the LGBTQ community, a demographic that had previously been critical of Chick-Fil-A and its outspoken owner, Dan Cathay, for his stand on same-sex marriage.[12]

However, these most recent efforts are relatively consistent with Chick-Fil-A's contemporary engagement with the LGBTQ market. Since Cathay's highly publicized comments, the restaurant and Cathay himself have tried purposely to remove the rift between themselves and their critics. Cathay, without retracting his statements, admitted that he had erred by subscribing his personal viewpoints to his professional enterprise, and in so doing had injudiciously alienated significant segments of the consumer market.[13] The organization also sought to distance itself from previous partners that were viewed as discriminatory and internally

---

[11] Richardson, B. (2016). Restaurants respond to Orlando massacre with free food at blood drives. *The Washington Times.*

[12] McGregor, J. (2012). CEO Dan Cathy steps into gay-marriage debate. *The Washington Post.*

[13] Stafford, L. (2014). Cathy seeks to put gay marriage flap behind . *The Atlanta Journal-Constitution.*

recognized its responsibility to respect all individuals, irrespective of sexual orientation.

While some may view Chick-Fil-A's actions as an insincere ploy, or even a cowardly capitulation, we perceive it as a synergistic response to the Christian responsibility to live by and promote biblical morality, and the Christian business leader's obligation to his or her job responsibilities. Whether one agrees with morality of gay marriage or not is not relevant here. What cannot be argued is the responsibility for Christians to engage in the discussions and debates on morality in general and biblical morality specifically. What must be considered for the business leader is the degree to which his or her statements are viewed as positions of the organization they represent. We don't know if Cathay's views on gay marriage changed or not. However, the wording of his apology and Chick-Fil-A's response to partners suggests that he understood that he could not subscribe his personal belief to the company in any way that could lead to discriminatory practices which would be immoral and illegal. As stated in the previous chapter on support and empowerment, the challenge for Christian leaders is creating a type of environment based on Christian principles where Christians and non-Christians are supported and empowered. Cathay's actions provide an example of, as well as the challenges created by leading in a space where faith, observable knowledge, philosophy, culture, and the law interact, by engaging in the debates and discussions of societal morality and meeting organizational responsibilities to Chick-Fil-A's diverse stakeholders. For believers that view Cathay's response purely as compromise, the critical question is what would be the alternative. Would it be better that voices like Cathay's not be in the room to bring the Christian perspective in the debates and discussions of societal morality? If Chick-Fil-A took a stand to not serve a community due to sin; what other communities should they not serve? Is it okay to do business with non-believers? Since all have sinned, would Chick-Fil-A have any customers? The view that synergistic strategy, that takes into account diverse stakeholders as well as observable knowledge, philosophy, culture, and law, is compromising the Gospel of Christ is simply not that simple.

We argue that the company's willingness to forego stringency with respect to a mindset and adopt synergy with respect to a market is aligned with the attitudes and actions of Christ. Jesus, on numerous occasions, courted controversy by contravening custom, including healing and gathering food on the Sabbath (Bible, Matt 12:9-14; Mark 3:1-6; Luke 6:6-11), and interacting intimately with those considered 'unclean' (Bible, John 4:7; Mark 2:15). In Sharon Ringe's interpretation of Sabbath observance, she examines the healing controversies bring attention to the debate regarding keeping specific Sabbath rules, versus how to make the day holy, which is what those rules were meant to assure.[14] While Ringe's examination demonstrates the complexity of this debate, one thing relevant to our

---

[14] Ringe, S., H. (2005). Holy, as the Lord Your God Commanded You: Sabbath in the New Testament. Interpretation: *A Journal of Bible and Theology, 59*, 17–24.

discussion is quite clear: No matter how clear or well-meaning rules are, there will be a need for exceptions. The complexity comes in determining boundaries for those exceptions. Jesus set broad boundaries by focusing on the purpose of Sabbath observance rather than the specifics. Jesus's aim through these contraventions was not to advocate for compromise, but to appeal for community; a goal Chick-Fil-A has seemingly favored in its contemporary beliefs and behaviors.

It's not only business organization that are faced with these types of dilemmas. Calvin University, a private evangelical college in Michigan, operated the Center for Social Research, a hub for social science research. Calvin has a prohibition of same sex marriages and had learned that a female employee at the center had married her girlfriend. The university had to use synergistic decision making to address the decision makers' own personal beliefs that God's word requires; multiple stakeholders including a growing number of students more supportive of LGBTQ relationships, board members that are more conservative toward religious traditions, and alumni that likely run the gambit of beliefs; and the legal implications involved Title IX specifically.[15] The final solution was an agreed upon, budget neutral split between the university and the center. Whether you agree with the outcome or not is not the issue here. What we hope to show is the necessity of synergy when dealing with multiple diverse and intersecting issues. In this case, Calvin University didn't change its rule, but severed a relationship to maintain it. Calvin University is part of the Council of Christian Colleges and Universities that, according to a spokesperson, aligns around the foundations of biblical truth, Christian formation, and gospel witness. The split nature of the reaction from Calvin students and alumni, from support to demand for change, demonstrates the degree to which many of our fellow Christians are at least reexamining traditional views of biblical truth, and the degree to which the works of Knust and other biblical scholars are directly challenging traditional interpretations of biblical truths. It is our belief that synergy will be more important for Calvin University moving forward than it was for this one employment case.

Another case to show that no organization is immune from diversity of thought, even if all sides of such thought is biblically and spiritually based, is that of the presidential election of the 2022 Southern Baptist Convention (SBC). There was significant disagreement on the degree that liberal drift was a significant issue for the convention and how to address a shocking report from Guidepost Solutions detailing how SBC leaders have handled widespread sexual abuse for the past two decades. Both moderate and conservative delegates believed their views were biblically based and were the right priorities for spreading the Gospel. The moderate candidate won the election, however 39% of the delegates voted with

---

[15] Whitford, E. (2022). *Calvin and Research Center split over LGBTQ rights. inside higher ed.* https://www.insidehighered.com/news/2022/03/28/calvin-spins-research-center-avoid-firing-gay-worker?utm_source=Inside+Higher+Ed&utm_campaign=fcee93492a-DNU_2021_COPY_02&utm_medium=email&utm_term=0_1fcbc04421-fcee93492a-199586697&mc_cid=fcee93492a&mc_eid=9b34401fb0

the conservative candidate, which demonstrates the variation in beliefs and opinions. The SBC is in itself a conservative denomination, so moderate may not be the best descriptor for Pastor Bart Barber, but a quote from one of his nominating delegates suggested the necessity for synergistic thinking within the SBC. Pastor Matt Henslee, from Texas, said about Barber "We need a man who can lead us through the battleground of our disagreements to the common ground of our co-operation." We suggest that synergistic thinking is necessary for this type of leadership. The concept of synergy allows all types of organizations, from for-profits, like Chick-Fil-A, to a religious governing body, like the SBC, to remain focused on their ideals but simultaneously flexible in their implementation to achieve their desired outcomes.

As we have demonstrated through this discourse, it is possible, and often practical to be spiritually purposeful and strategically prudent, and that immovable precepts and policies may actually endanger the outcome of virtuous leadership. Alternatively, we suggest that systematically synergizing with market movements is likely to be more effective in upholding the tenets of Christian leadership but also in sharing these tenets with a wider, more diverse audience.

CHAPTER 7

CONCLUSION

Subsidiarity, Stewardship, Service, Support and Synergy can all be treated as religious tenets but we have purposely considered how these are contrasted with past considerations and how they are best operationalized in a contemporary environment, while still maintaining their moralistic impetus and connection to Christianity.

Final chapters often pose a particular dilemma for authors. Should they serve as an effective and influential summary that reiterates the significant and unique contributions of the piece, or should they focus the reader's consideration firmly on how best to utilize this research for future benefit? We choose to concentrate on the latter, primarily because our motivation for this work continues to be found in our desire to make operational and available constructs such as spirituality, and more importantly, Christian leadership and strategy to a diverse spectrum of organizational leaders.

Again, we posit that this book is not written exclusively for businesses and business owners that already consider themselves as practitioners of Christ like management. Admittedly, we anticipate that this audience may consider our offerings repetitive and potentially even controversial. Instead, we have attempted to build a framework, biblically based and strategically sound, that appeals to an audience seeking a competitive advantage, while remaining true to, or contributing to its faith.

Strategy in His Image: Supporting and Sustaining Organizational Strategy
From a Christian Perspective, pages 47–49.
Copyright © 2023 by Information Age Publishing
www.infoagepub.com

Each of our four elements is rooted in scriptural foundations but we have been intentional in discussing tangible ways that the Bible and business not only co-exist, but also are congruent. Subsidiarity, Stewardship, Service, Support, and Synergy can all be treated as religious tenets, but we have purposely considered how these are contrasted with past considerations and how they are best operationalized in a contemporary environment, while still maintaining their moralistic impetus and connection to Christianity. For example, Subsidiarity is neither decentralization of management nor apostleship; it borrows and benefits from both, residing at the interface of participatory leadership and Christian initiative.

The advantage of positioning something in a novel manner, Subsidiarity in this case, is that we do not, inadvertently or otherwise, create unnecessary contention between the secular and the sacred. We are not trying to 'Christianize' a conventional business concept or even share why a 'Jesus' approach is superior. Alternatively, we argue what 'Jesus' leadership looks like scripturally and how it can be best implemented, especially alongside a culture of organizational solidarity, to give avenue for personal purpose without sacrificing corporate commitment.

Similarly, in our treatment of synergy, we are not simply repacking something like conscious capitalism. We do suggest that markets and morality find overlap, but further argue that perceived conflicts between doing good ethically and doing well financial may be removed by the biblical record and a contextual examination of Christ's actions. Thus, we do not seek Christian compromise or organizational compliance. We recognize that morality has and will continue to impact market mechanisms, but we are less interested in virtuous economics. Our premise is that organizational leaders must appreciate both organizations and Christianity as institutions with missions and motives towards the common good. Of course, these entities have evolved differently and separately, but historical assessment will defend the statement that the church and commerce have been and always will be intrinsically involved. Therefore, we desire a shift away from 'forcing' the church on corporations or 'forcing' faith out of corporations towards a shared value and virtue approach that requires all of us to come and reason together.

Moving forward, this theme of integration is also considered in how these elements work together and reinforce each other. While we imply that subsidiarity, stewardship, support, and synergy interact and possess common elements, we presume that firms can practice and/or prioritize each separately. Subsidiarity undoubtedly does not require synergy, but a transition that includes and invests in the individual, that may also help the firm to be more welcoming to stakeholder and social integration. This encourages a richer and more empirical analysis of the direction, duality, dimension, and diversity of these four forces that unfortunately resides outside the scope of this book. However, it is, in our opinion, a decisive next step forward as we continue to refine our model pragmatically.

Beyond model examination, our greatest hope is to bridge and build conversation. As authors, we have debated between ourselves exactly who might be most interested and gain the greatest utility from this book. Although we unapologetically base much of our material on biblical passages, the book's imperative and application reside primarily outside the church walls. But rather than segmenting its contents to satisfy separate audiences, it is our sincere prayer that pastors and practitioners alike will consume all, and from this be inspired to share and shape new schema in the Christian space, specifically, and spirituality space, in general. This is our initial contribution to this encouraging future.

AUTHORS

Dr. Joe M. Ricks, Jr., is the J.P. Morgan Chase Professor of Sales & Marketing at Xavier University of Louisiana. Dr. Ricks earned a Ph.D. in marketing with a minor in cognitive psychology for Louisiana State University, a Masters of Business Administration from the University of New Orleans and a Bachelors degree in Marketing from Southeastern Louisiana University. Professionally, Dr. Ricks has published in many business related journals including Business and Society Review, Industrial Marketing Management, the European Journal of Marketing, the Journal of Business Ethics, and others. Along with his work on Christian principle for business strategy he is currently conducting research examining how marketing can increase African American participation in clinical trials. Dr. Ricks has been a visiting professor at 3M Company in St. Paul Minnesota and at Young & Rubicam Advertising Agency in New York. He has also been a marketing intern coordinator for McIllhenny Company maker of Tabasco. Currently he serves on the board of the New Orleans Center for Creative Arts, the Friends of Fisher House of Southern Louisiana, the Louisiana Quality Foundation that awards the Louisiana Performance Excellence award based on the Malcolm Baldrige quality criteria, and he is a past Chairman of the City of New Orleans Ethics Review Board, and past President of the National HBCU Business Deans

Strategy in His Image: Supporting and Sustaining Organizational Strategy From a Christian Perspective, pages 51–52.
Copyright © 2023 by Information Age Publishing
www.infoagepub.com

Roundtable. Dr. Ricks is a husband, father, veteran of the United States Army and is a member of the Franklin Avenue Baptist Church.

Dr. Richard Peters earned a Bsc. (1st Class Honors) from the University of West Indies in Chemistry & Management. He has a Master's of Business Administration from Pace University and a PhD. In Strategic Management from Florida Atlantic University. Richard presently serves as an Associate Dean of the College of Arts and Sciences at Xavier University of Louisiana. His research interests are in Corporate Social Responsibility and Sustainability (CSRS) with an emphasis on social innovation and Christian Leadership. He has published articles in business-related journals and has presented at numerous international, national, and regional conferences. He is a reviewer for academic journals and an associate editor of Business and Society Review. Dr. Peters sits on the advisory board of the Global Jesuit Case Series and is a board member for the Society for Case Research. He is also passionate about bringing impactful change to communities and environments. He has worked with colleagues, organizations, and students on issues related to social responsibility and sustainability and has participated locally as well as internationally to promote social responsibility and sustainability education and efforts. Dr. Peters is a husband, father and remains a proud 'Trinbagonian.'